Contents

*Commitment and
Community*

─────Commitment and Community

GEORGE RUPP

Fortress Press   Minneapolis

——— *For Erika*
Nancy
Kathy and Stephanie

Library of Congress Cataloging-in-Publication Data

Rupp, George.
    Commitment and community.

    Includes index.
    1. Religious pluralism.   2. Commitment (Psychology)—
Religious aspects.   3. Religious communities.   4. Reli-
gion and sociology.   5. Religions.   I. Title.
BL85.R83   1989   306.6   89-12036
ISBN 0-8006-2332-0

Manufactured in the U.S.A.   AF 1–2332

93   92   91   90   89   1   2   3   4   5   6   7   8   9   10

Preface

I argue in this book that contemporary commitment is most adequate when it is grounded in the traditions of a particular community and at the same time relates constructively both to other communities and to the broader society. This position is advanced as a coherent alternative to various and often overlapping forms of inadequacy: retreat to private preference, authoritarian assertion, uncritical legitimation of established patterns, reduction to a least common denominator. In contrast to such inadequacies, commitment today can and should integrate the power sustained in and expressed through particular communities with responsible participation in a pluralistic world.

This book comprises a series of variations on this theme of commitment and community. Each chapter is a revised version of an article or lecture initially developed in response to a specific invitation. Had the invitations been different, the particular topics addressed would no doubt also have varied. The underlying theme of commitment and community nonetheless informs the project as a whole and each of its parts. As is evident from my summary characterization of the theme of the book and the organization of the chapters, I examine commitment in relation to a plurality of traditions and to public issues in the broader society. The two sets of relationships cannot simply be separated, as is clear in the recurrent turn to social issues in the first four chapters. But the two-part structure of the book identifies distinguishable challenges and orders the chapters according to whether intellectual or institutional issues are the focus of attention.

Seven of the chapters are revised versions of essays also published elsewhere: chapter 1 as "Commitment in a Pluralistic World," in *Religious Pluralism*, ed. Leroy S. Rouner (Notre Dame, Ind.: University of Notre Dame Press, 1984), 214–26; chapter 3 as "Incarnation and Apocalyptic: Christology in the Context of Religious Pluralism," *Word and World*, 3 (Winter 1983): 41–50; chapter 4 as

"The Critical Appropriation of Traditions: Theology and the Comparative History of Religion," in *The World's Religious Traditions: Essays in Honour of Wilfred Cantwell Smith*, ed. Frank Whaling (Edinburgh: T & T Clark, 1984), 165–80; chapter 5 as "The Changing Role of Religion in Society," *Harvard Divinity Bulletin* 14 (December 1983–January 1984): 12–16; chapter 6 as "Communities of Faith/Communities of Learning," in *Faith and Reason in Higher Education: Vision and Tradition for the New University*, ed. Charles B. Vedder (DeLand, Fla.: Stetson University, 1983), 37–45, and also as a few paragraphs in my *Beyond Existentialism and Zen: Religion in a Pluristic World* (New York: Oxford University Press, 1979), 7-9; chapter 7 as "From Civil Religion to Public Faith," in *On the Way: Occasional Papers of the Wisconsin Conference of the United Church of Christ* 3/1 (Summer 1985): 23–35, and also in the forthcoming *Religion and Politics*, ed. Andrew R. Cecil and W. Lawson Taitte (Dallas: University of Texas, 1989); chapter 8 as "Preparing for the 21st Century: Beyond Complacency and Nostalgia," in *Texas Journal of Ideas, History and Culture*, 11/2 (Spring-Summer 1989): 4–7. I acknowledge with gratitude permission from or prior agreement with those publishers and journals to include copyrighted materials in this book.

The context in which I wrote most of this book is Harvard's Divinity School and its Center for the Study of World Religions. This setting embodies not only in individual but also in institutional terms the struggle to integrate the power of particular commitment with responsible participation in a pluralistic world. I am deeply grateful to student, faculty, and administrative colleagues and friends who shared interest in and also pressed engagement with the issues I address, in particular among them James Luther Adams, Constance Buchanan, John Carman, Harvey Cox, Elizabeth Dodson Gray, Paul Hanson, Gordon Kaufman, Margaret Miles, Richard Niebuhr, Sharon Parks, Lamin Sanneh, and Wilfred Cantwell Smith.

I am thankful as well to colleagues who helped with the preparation of multiple versions of the individual essays and then the book in its entirety: to the late Elizabeth d'Estree, Barbara Driver, and Lucy Daley when they and I were at Harvard and Jackie Bourne and Lisa Gilbreath at Rice for typing and word processing; and to J. Michael West, now of Fortress Press, whose persistence was instrumental in the move from discrete pieces to publication as a single work.

The book is dedicated with heartfelt gratitude to four members of my immediate family who have fundamentally shaped my own commitments and who constitute my closest community: my mother Erika, my wife Nancy, and our daughters Kathy and Stephanie.

—George Rupp

PART ONE

Commitment in the Context of Pluralism

———— 1

Commitment as Appropriation of Traditions

We live in an era when the traditional foundations for faith are severely shaken. In a sense, the Protestant principle has triumphed. No individual or institution has unquestioned authority.

In an extension of this Protestant principle beyond what the Reformers themselves envisioned, certainly the authority of the Bible itself has not gone unquestioned. Impressive numbers of people may still insist that they accept the Bible as the inerrant authority for their faith. Similarly, significant numbers of the faithful declare their submission to the teaching authority of the church— to the Magisterium and to the Pope when he speaks ex cathedra. But the need to interpret and adapt authoritative pronouncements in their everyday application characterizes the behavior of even those who subscribe to inerrant authority in principle. Think of fundamentalist interpretations of the Sermon on the Mount that somehow still support American superpatriotism. Or consider birth control among devout Roman Catholics. In short, no authority remains unquestioned in practice.

The situation is analogous to that of true believers in the political realm. In recent years there has been no shortage of declarations of support for the United States Constitution as virtually sacrosanct. And yet every position on the political spectrum has its recommendations for improvement. In some instances, the proposed amendment is quite self-consciously advanced to rectify limitations in the time-bound and partial vision of the framers of the Constitution. The Equal Rights Amendment is a case in point. In other instances the change is presented as consistent with the intention of the framers of the Constitution; so the amendment is offered as a more specific application designed to address new issues and to counter intervening misinterpretations of fundamental rights. The proposal for a constitutional amendment to ban state support for abortions illustrated this pattern. But in each case, the effect is to propose amendment in what is a foundational authority of American political life.

Because we discount the excesses of political rhetoric, we are not overly surprised at the proposing of Constitutional amendments. After all, we know that there have been more than a few formal amendments and that there will be more over the years. But in our religious communities, there is no similarly formalized procedure for amending the pronouncements of our foundational authorities. Nor is there a formally established record of those amendments over time. As a result, change in our religious traditions strikes us less as a process of orderly amendment and more as a shaking of the very foundations of faith.

THE RELATIVIZING OF RELIGIOUS AUTHORITY

That there are changes in our religious traditions is certainly not a new development. Changes in belief and practice have occurred in the course of the history of all religious communities—even the most tenaciously conservative ones. But our sense of the shaking of the foundations of faith has an edge to it that distinguishes our situation from much of the past. The reason is that we are crossing the threshold into a new era in the history of human religious life. What characterizes this new era is an increasingly general recognition of our individual and corporate role in fashioning the religious worlds, the symbolic universes, in which we live.

Awareness of this role is not unprecedented. Exceptional individuals—both critics of religion and initiates in its mysteries—have for millenia insisted on this dynamic contribution of the human imagination to religious traditions. An intriguing Western example is the quite self-conscious recasting of Greek mythology in the late drama of Euripides. And in the East, both elaborate symbolic inventiveness and vigorous iconoclasm are evident among initiates in, for example, tantric or Zen Buddhism.

What is new in our situation is that not only exceptional individuals but also prevailing cultural movements are coming to recognize our collective role in fashioning religious symbols. The threshold into this new era is admittedly a pretty wide one. In the West, we have been in the process of crossing it for at least several centuries. But the shift from the insight of exceptional individuals to a cultural ethos of general recognition is nonetheless a profoundly challenging transition for religious communities.

The challenge may be formulated quite simply. Are religious communities viable in this new situation of increased self-consciousness? Can religious communities survive in this situation? For those of us who are their members, religious communities provide symbolic universes: rituals, injunctions, images, and ideas through which we interpret and in turn shape our experience. The question is whether we can continue to live within such a symbolic universe once we recognize its status as a creation of collective human insight and imagination.

The force of this question in our personal and cultural awareness is accentuated by changes in the social location of religion. In the institutionally least complex cultures about which we have data, there is no differentiation of a religious group from the society as a whole. Instead, the tribe is a single political-economic-religious entity. In more complex societies, religious institutions typically are differentiated from political and economic ones. The priest and the king are no longer the same person. In the terms of Christian tradition, in which this differentiation has become sharpest and most self-conscious, there is a church distinguished from the state. But separation of church and state as two more or less unified spheres mutually balancing and correcting each other is not the final stage in this line of development. Instead, as the process of differentiation continues, the dichotomy of state and church yields to a series of regions or dimensions of society that mutually influence each other: not only the political and the religious, but also the economic, the educational, the legal, the artistic, and so on.

The result of this process of differentiation is a sense of movement of religious communities toward the periphery of the social system. Religious life is not inescapably integral to our very existence as social beings, as in tribal culture. Nor is a unified religious community institutionalized as one of two central authorities that structure the social system, as in medieval Europe, for example. Instead, religious communities are among those voluntary associations to which we may belong as we struggle to orient our lives, appraise competing value systems, and commit ourselves to the causes that seem most compelling.

Viewed from the perspective of traditional religious authority, our situation is, then, doubly dubious: individuals are more and more aware of their role in shaping religious traditions; and religious communities are increasingly marginal in the social system as a whole. The two developments reinforce each other. The result is that our religious life is beset with the same dispirited individualism that plagues so much of contemporary society. Even those of us who affirm religious values as crucial to our identities may do so apart from any commitment to a self-consciously religious community. We Americans have a two-hundred-year tradition in support of this tendency. In the words of Thomas Paine, "My mind is my church"; or, as Thomas Jefferson put it, "I am a sect myself."[1] A religious dimension of the culture that is available directly to individuals displaces religious institutions. Here, as elsewhere in our society, individualism threatens to run amok.

An effective response in this situation must engage the issues focused in modern Western individualism. I see this need as a religious imperative: central to the religious life is the struggle against our idolatrous glorification of the self. But the need to address the issue of unchecked individualism also follows from considerations of social psychology and the sociology of knowledge. Thomas Paine and Thomas Jefferson to the contrary notwithstanding, every person is not and cannot be his or her own church.

In part because religious communities are no longer centrally and unquestionably authoritative in contemporary society, we do have an increased awareness of our role in shaping the symbolic universes in which we live. But we do not simply invent our symbols. Instead, we participate in changing traditions and therefore bear responsibility for the ongoing development of the symbolic resources available through those traditions. In some cases, it may be most responsible simply to reject a tradition. Even then we are not, however, moving out of every symbolic universe. Nor are we creating an entirely new one. Instead, we are engaged in a process of critical appropriation through which we assess and often reinterpret the symbols available to us, even as we make them our own and live out of them.

To focus this general description of what I am calling critical appropriation of traditions, I will sketch two contemporary illustrations of the process involved. The first is the impact of feminism on contemporary religious life and thought. The second is the religious and ethical challenge of limits to growth in our biosphere.

THE IMPACT OF FEMINISM

The impact of feminism has made us painfully aware of how deeply patriarchal are the symbolic forms and institutional patterns of Jewish and Christian traditions. In the most categorical expression of this sexism, women are simply barred from positions of authority in the liturgical and administrative life of the community. But even when this extreme is rejected, the sexism that pervades the language and imagery of churches and synagogues remains. Those of us who have tried to locate biblical texts, liturgies, or hymns that do not have sexually exclusive language know how pervasive is this sexism in virtually every aspect of our religious traditions.

For significant numbers of contemporary Christians and Jews, this pervasive presence of sexist language and imagery is simply unacceptable. It is unacceptable in the straightforward sense that it interferes with the very act of worship. Instead of being incorporated into a vital community that transcends the individual, we experience exclusion that vitiates any sense of a common and inclusive body.

This contemporary state of affairs is very much a product of historical development. For thousands of years, participants in biblical traditions have been able to celebrate their common life without being conscious of the sexism that pervades those traditions. That third-person singular masculine pronouns and nouns like *man* and *mankind* are intended as inclusive in reference was for our forebears a grammatical point that did not violate their conscious experience. Similarly, references to God as masculine were not perceived to be dignifying male as distinguished from female experience. But that is no longer the case for increasing numbers of women and men. In sum, authoritative traditions have come into direct conflict with our contemporary awareness of the role of gender in the symbolization and institutionalization of religious life.

In theory, we can envision three ideal typical responses to this situation. One is to insist on the inviolability of the authoritative traditions and therefore to reject the claims of contemporary aware-ness as illegitimate human self-exaltation. A second is to reject completely the pretentions of the tradition and to affirm the new awareness as alone having true authority—as exercising genuine power in our common life. The third response is to recognize that neither authoritative traditions nor contemporary awareness can be rejected completely and that, therefore, there is no alternative except to attempt to do justice to the power of both.

As this formulation suggests, the three theoretical responses in practice are points on a single spectrum. Even the most conservative traditions change over time; and even the most unqualifed com-mitment to radically novel insight or awareness draws on the re-sources of the past. Responses to a specific issue may fall at multiple points on the spectrum. But none of them can fail to take a position with reference to both poles. To adapt an aphorism from Kant: fidelity to tradition without attention to contemporary experience is empty; exaltation of current awareness apart from the symbolic resources of the past is blind.

Specifically on the issues focused in contemporary feminism, a full spectrum of responses is represented. It ranges from modest renovation among those who want to continue to dwell in the house of traditional authority through efforts at more systemic transfor-mation to emphatic rejection of Christian traditions in their entirety. But in each case, there is the recognition of the need for at least some changes and there is also, despite protestations to the con-trary, very substantial continuity. Commitment "beyond God the Father" is still heavily dependent on theological and philosophical images and ideas fundamentally shaped in Western patriarchal traditions.[2]

In exemplifying the process of critical appropriation through which we assess and often reinterpret the symbols available to us, the feminist movement also illustrates the complex relationship between Western individualism and the increased self-conscious-ness about commitment today. In a sense, the movement in its contemporary form is itself a powerful expression of just this in-dividualism. After centuries of accepting and affirming identities that subordinated their individuality to the prerogatives of others, women have insisted that they, too, must be able to do their own thing. At the same time, the feminist movement has had the greatest impact when it in effect provides a community in which this new individuality is nourished and sustained. The broader culture can and does offer various stimuli to individuals, especially through the mass media. But this general cultural awareness is certainly not as effective in enabling change as is a community of shared commitment in support of that change.

In this respect also, the feminist movement exemplifies the general issues involved in contemporary commitment. Talk of assessing alternatives and reinterpreting traditional symbolism unavoidably sounds highly individualistic. But that process of critical appraisal in turn shapes our living most effectively when we participate in a community that shares our commitment. Through this active collaboration, both the symbolic resources of the tradition and the participants are changed.

THE IMPLICATIONS OF LIMITS TO GROWTH

Like the impact of feminism, the second illustration I will sketch— the challenge of limits to growth in our biosphere—also has implications for both the symbolization and the institutionalization of our common life. In short, this challenge also affects both our ideas and our actions.

It is, I think, helpful to view the impact on religious life in historical perspective. Most of the traditional forms of what have become the great world religions generate their power through appeal to a realm or an order of reality that is construed as the ultimate destiny of the human and in comparison to which this historical existence is radically deficient or even hopelessly corrupt. In much Christian piety, this realm is heaven over against earth or the liberating vision of God over against enslavement to the world. In Islam even more than in Christianity, the conception of God as utterly transcendent is central; and, valued as is this temporal life, it is for the devout Muslim infinitely inferior to the life to come, which alone is enduring. For the Theravada Buddhist, this destiny is the attainment of the other shore, of *nirvana* over against *samsara*; for the Pure Land Buddhist, it is rebirth in the western paradise of Amida. For virtually all Hindus, the goal of the religious life is the attainment of *moksha*: deliverance from the round of birth and death that constitutes ordinary historical life.

In popular piety, deliverance to this other realm—heaven, *nirvana,* the pure land, union with the ultimate through release from recurrent births—is often portrayed as the destiny of the faithful, disciplined, or devoted individual. In the various religious traditions there are, however, also resources for interpreting this deliverance in less individualistic terms. Liberation from Egypt and possession of the promised land are dramatic instances of corporate and this-worldly deliverance in biblical faith. So too are certain Mahayana Buddhist tendencies—for example, the vow of the *bodhisattva* to save all sentient beings rather than attain deliverance alone. But the predominant pattern is that such corporate or inclusive transformation is projected into the future, enacted in an apocalyptic end time, or realized apart from all ordinary historical processes. In the end there is a transforming resurrection of all humankind. Or, in a final vindication of divine power, the kingdom of God is established in utter discontinuity with human historical development. Or, through rigorous spiritual discipline, enlightenment is attained and all of reality is seen to be Buddha-nature— even though to ordinary human vision it is unchanged. Or, through renunciation of worldly involvements, the transtemporal identity of the self with the ultimate is realized in a single all-comprehending whole. In sum, even though in such instances the goal of the religious life is envisioned as a reality that transcends the individual, its realization is still viewed as discontinuous with ordinary historical life.

To this pattern of traditional religion in both its individual and universal forms, the post–Enlightenment West has posited a direct and quite simple alternative: human progress. The goal of human life is not envisioned as discontinuous with history. Instead, human history itself is presumed to be progressing inexorably into, or at least is thought to be developing toward, ever greater fulfillment. Like the pattern of traditional religion, this alternative is expressed in both individualistic and corporate forms, as is illustrated in the numerous versions of bourgeois individualism and Marxism. But in all of the variations, transformation discontinuous with ordinary life is replaced with hope for the future of human development. The vision of heaven above is translated into aspirations for the earth below.

Although it has been severely shaken by the cataclysms of our century, this presumption of continuing progress is still central to the cultural ethos of much of the West. It is a salient feature in the ideology of both laissez-faire capitalism and Marxism. It certainly has shaped the rhetoric and also the programs of parties at all points on the political spectrum. In alliance with traditional tendencies to ethical perfectionism and spiritual discipline, commitment to progress has also found expression in religious and philanthropic communities, as dedication to human welfare has become a goal significant in its own right rather than a temporary means to transtemporal salvation for both the donor and the recipient.

Because the presumption of progress has been central to so many post-Enlightenment cultural traditions, it unavoidably informs our current discussions of limits to growth in the biosphere. Indeed, those discussions become traumatic precisely because the very idea of limits to growth seems to contradict the tenet of indefinitely extended progress still central to much of our culture.

At first glance, threats to the ideology of progress might appear to signal a revival of what I have called the pattern of traditional religion. After all, the attractiveness of traditionally valued forms of religious development is only enhanced with the recognition that indefinite material progress cannot be sustained. Striving toward ethical improvement and disciplined spiritual attainment do not depend on the exploitation of limited resources. From this perspective, only the illegitimate secularized versions of religion that focus on this-worldly welfare are shown to be untenable. Traditional religion, in contrast, is vindicated through its refusal to compromise with secular culture in its preoccupation with material progress.

Despite the so-called moral majority and, in general, the resurgence of conservative religion, the situation is not that simple. The preoccupation of the post–Enlightenment West with progress is not simply an aberration. Nor does the impending collapse of that preoccupation signal a return to the simple truths of traditional religion. We are all children of the Enlightenment who cannot simply return to the comforting dualisms of traditional religion. Instead, for most of us, too, visions of heaven have come to represent hopes for our common life here on earth. To use Buddhist imagery, the land of Amida Buddha is our historical life transformed and purified.

Like the proponents of progress, we yearn for a transformation in the personal, social, and cultural dimensions of our common life in history. But that transformation cannot be envisioned as only a future realization of all the ideals and aspirations that motivate present action. Instead, we also at least inchoately participate now in the corporate reality to which the symbols of religious traditions testify: in Christian imagery, the reality of spirit, the kingdom or commonwealth of God, the divine-human body of which we are all members.

For those of us who cannot return to the dualisms of traditional religion, there is a special urgency and also a sense of tragedy in our appropriation of such symbols of human destiny. This double sense of urgency and tragedy embraces not only the individual but also humanity as a whole, and, indeed, all of life as we know it. Many of us cannot affirm individual survival of death in some other realm. As a result, we place a special premium on the contributions we are enabled to make and the satisfactions we are allowed to enjoy in all the dimensions of our daily living. A similar sense of tragedy and urgency seems to envelop our corporate existence. That is, there appears to be a final limit to the viability of the earth as an ecosystem capable of supporting life as we know it. So our corporate life also is lived in the face of a final death that accentuates the need to realize value here and now.

In this context of limits to growth in our biosphere and even a final term to the viability of our ecosystem, to affirm that we are all members of one body has definite implications for action. Any such affirmation calls for measures to redress the enormously uneven distribution of wealth that makes a mockery of all talk about an inclusive human community. And the fact that available resources are limited serves to accentuate the indefensibility of dramatically inequitable distribution. The easy answers of the recent past become less and less plausible: proportionately the same slices of an ever larger socioeconomic pie may have some attractions even to those with small pieces; but if the pie cannot increase in size indefinitely or even for very long, then the alternative of reslicing it becomes compelling.

In sum, in the context of limits to growth, our appropriation of such religious images as the spiritual community, the kingdom or commonwealth of God, and the divine-human body of which we are all members entails a commitment to programs of redistribution rather than the easy gradualism that assumes indefinitely extended socioeconomic growth. As we move increasingly to an integrated planetary culture, we must, therefore, press for policies that protect and further the interests of the Third World. Similarly, we must struggle toward institutional patterns that reinforce simplicity and frugality rather than unnecessary production and consumption. Only through this double movement toward reduced consumption and redistribution of wealth can we be faithful to affirmations of inclusive community.

THE CHALLENGE OF APPROPRIATION

The need for redistribution of resources in the context of limits to growth is not as directly a personal challenge as are the issues at the heart of the feminist critique. Yet both challenges call for a fundamental change that must begin as particular communities actualize new or reaffirmed values in their common life. In both cases, there is a general cultural awareness of the need for this change. But also in both cases, the call for change is most effective when there is a community of shared commitment in support of that change.

The examples of the feminist movement and the limits to growth in our biosphere in effect pose the question: Where is this community of mutual support to be located? More specifically, can it be located within religious communities?

This question brings us full circle to the issues involved in the collapse of traditional authorities. Not only the traditional foundations for faith but also other authorities are shaken. Yet the reverberations of the collapse seem especially pronounced in the case of religious communities. Religious life has so powerfully shaped human identities at least in part because it has engaged the deepest levels of the self at the earliest and perhaps the most formative stages of development. For precisely that reason, increased self-consciousness about our individual and corporate role in fashioning our symbolic universes constitutes a particularly fundamental shift in this case.

For several centuries in the West, the presumption has been that the recognition of religious symbols as human artifacts requires a rejection of those symbols. But we have also come to see that we unavoidably live within one symbolic universe or another. Thus a rejection of religious symbols does not itself settle the issue of what values we commit ourselves to or what meanings we affirm. Conversely, even in the wake of the collapse of traditional authorities, religious communities may well survive if they conduct genuine power to their members—if they provide a context in which individuals are delivered from their self-preoccupations for commitment to more inclusive causes. To this end, the rituals, injunctions, images, and ideas of particular communities must be represented effectively so that they both interpret the full range of contemporary experience and in turn shape that experience in ways that elicit affirmation.

This need is not just the expression of an abstract intellectual interest. Instead, it directly affects our lives in all of their empirical concreteness. To refer again to the two illustrations I sketched, the issues focused in the feminist challenge to religious imagery and institutions affect not only our ideas but also our most fundamental individual and corporate identities. Similarly, our increased awareness of limits to growth in our biosphere affects every dimension of our living. Consequently, interpretations of contemporary experience through reference to traditional images and ideas must in turn shape our lives in ways that we affirm. In the case of the feminist challenge, we must realize the potential in biblical and other religious traditions for supporting inclusive communities that enhance the female as well as the male dimensions of the human. And in the instance of limits to growth, we must come to affirm our situation as finite moments integral to an order of being and value that has the capacity to be inclusive and just.

The need to relate traditional symbols to contemporary life is certainly not a new imperative for religious communities. But our greater self-consciousness about this process of appropriation has both a threatening and a promising aspect. Our new awareness can inhibit or even block the energy generated through religious commitment. We can become self-conscious in the debilitating sense of looking only at ourselves and exaggerating our role as individual arbiters or even manipulators of traditional symbols. But recognition of the role of human insight and imagination in fashioning our religious worlds can also be liberating. It can release both our critical and our creative capacities as we seek to act out of a corporate vision that we are committed to making our own. Because we recognize our responsibility for this process, we must identify those places in the tradition that do not adequately interpret and acceptably shape our experience. We must enlarge those places so that they can accommodate all that we affirm. Only this inclusive commitment can be at one and the same time faithful to the past, adequate for orienting us in the present, and promising in projecting us and our world into the future.

——— 2

Community and Divinity

In this chapter, I will again press into service the examples of feminist criticism and limits to growth. I do so because they not only illustrate the process of critical appropriation of traditions but also indicate how this process bears on even the most central and cherished convictions—in this case the commitment at the heart of theology, the affirmation of God. The issues entailed in the question of limits to growth in our biosphere are germane because the conception of progress has in effect served as a secular substitute for God. Similarly, feminist criticism of religious language is relevant both in its own right and because it expresses with renewed vigor and emotional power questions at the core of Christian theological traditions that for too long have been largely suppressed or treated in exclusively intellectual terms.

GOD THE FATHER AND THE IDEA OF PROGRESS

In our Western monotheistic traditions, God has persistently been conceived or visualized as a being who is above or outside the world. God is, to be sure, affirmed as the provident sustainer and governor of creation. Indeed, God is represented as concerned for, even as loving, the world. But this divine creator, king and ruler of the universe, and stern yet also caring father is represented in the religious imagination and also in the broader culture as over against the world. Thus, affirmation of monotheism has been assimilated to and has in turn reinforced an underlying dualism between God and the world, heaven and earth, spirit and matter, perhaps also male and female.

A deep historical irony—and also a profound truth—of Christianity is that while it has contributed enormous ideational and institutional power to this kind of dualism, it also carries at its heart a fundamental repudiation of every such position. Against the prevailing tendency of the philosophy of its day, what became the dominant Western Christian tradition declared that the divine was directly and intimately involved with creation. That was a crucial issue in the christological debates of the early centuries of Christian history. Was an intermediary being, more than human but less than fully divine, the mediator between God and humanity? Or was what Gnostic and neo-Platonic philosophy thought inconceivable nonetheless to be affirmed, namely, that God was fully present and active in this world? In declaring as orthodox this radical position— that is, in affirming the incarnation of God in the world—Christianity in principle broke with every final dualism. Indeed, in affirming God as infinite, as unbounded, as not limited, so to speak, from the outside, monotheism of every tradition also in principle rejects every dualism that sets God over against the world. And yet, despite this rejection in principle, Christian traditions have contributed to the persistent tendency across religious communities to identify religious faith or devotion or discipline with an underlying dualism between God and the world or the ultimate and the historical.

A deep stratum in the underlying concepts and characteristic images of God that we inherit is, then, the notion of the divine as a being outside or over against the world. In Western traditions, such concepts and images of God have certainly been patriarchal. God has been conceived as an individual being who transcends the world, and that being has been represented in predominantly if not exclusively male terms—father, not parent or mother; king, not queen; and so on. There is, therefore, a double problem: first, that the divine has been construed as an individual entity over against the world, with the support for underlying dualisms that this conception entails; and second, that this divinity has been construed as male, with all of the reinforcement of patriarchal social roles and institutional patterns that this fact implies.

The conception of God as a being beyond the world who rules or governs the created order and may on occasion also intervene in that order—this conception of God that is still the predominant representation of the divine in conventionally accepted religion—has of course been the focus of critical scrutiny for more than a little while. At least since the eighteenth century, God as so conceived has become increasingly dubious for increasing numbers of people. So, in a sense, this patriarchal concept of God has been dying a slow death for some time. As is the habit of our media, this several-hundred-year development became an ostensibly novel sensation in the 1960s when the so-called death-of-God theologians hit the headlines. But even the declaration "God is dead" traces back through Friedrich Nietzsche at least to G. W. F. Hegel, who used it in several works—both *Faith and Knowledge* and *The Phenomenology of Spirit*—written at the turn of the nineteenth century.[1] It is worth remembering what Nietzsche has Zarathustra think after he meets the old man in the forest in the prologue to *Thus Spake Zarathustra*:

> When Zarathustra was alone, however, he said to his heart: "Could it be possible! This old saint in the forest has not yet heard of it, that *God is dead!*"[2]

But even if this conception of God as a being beyond the world has been dying a slow death for some time, he has not been without his substitutes, most notably the modern Western conception of progress. Expressed in its self-consciously secular form at the height of the self-confidence of Enlightenment humanism, the idea of progress initially served as a nontheological alternative to the doctrine of divine providence. But in time, it was for many pressed into service to do double duty as a substitute for immortality as well. In this view, the goal of human life is not envisaged as discontinuous with history. Instead, human history itself is presumed to be progressing toward both individual and corporate fulfillment.

The substitution of progress for God has addressed and reformulated but not resolved the double problem confronting our underlying conceptions of the divine. It has rejected the conception of God as a being outside the world. But it has continued the pervasive patriarchal tendencies of the theology it rejects, as is indicated in the premium it places on technical manipulation and control and on orientation to the future. Furthermore, despite its continuing influence, the idea of progress, like belief in God as a being beyond the world, has become increasingly dubious to increasing numbers of people. Not only does the enormity of human evil in this century undercut optimism about progress at least in any value-laden sense of the term. Now also sobering projections as to the limits to growth sustainable in a biosphere of finite resources throw into doubt progressive programs that presuppose increases in goods sufficient to allow improvement in the prospects for all without decline in the situation of any.

This uncertain fate of the idea of progress is not simply a matter of the becoming dubious of one more isolated conception. Instead, this idea is a central organizing principle of a powerful world view that has dominated modern secular culture and much of post-Enlightenment religious thought as well. As a result, decreasing confidence in human capabilities and in the capacities of the environment to sustain progress toward what is affirmed as a better world is a significant indicator of and contributor to the loss of assurance of the modern West.

This loss of assurance is for our broader culture what erosion of belief in God as a being beyond the world is for conventional religion. In the latter instance we face the demise of an explicitly patriarchal concept of consciously affirmed deity. In the former case we witness the collapse of a God-substitute with only implicitly patriarchal characteristics. The two developments taken together may be understood to represent concepts of the ultimate that are in any case highly problematical on conceptual grounds but that now are also subject to vigorous and affectively powerful criticisms like those exemplified in feminist and environmental movements.

DIVINITY WITHOUT PATRIARCHY
OR PROGRESSIVISM

In this situation of emerging from and moving beyond patriarchal images and concepts of God, do we, then, experience a reality that we may name as divine? Is there a divine reality beyond "God the Father"?

Even when we address what we take to be divine reality as personal and employ representations from interpersonal life in our efforts to grasp or communicate what we experience as divine influence on us, even when we express our affirmations through such personal images and ideas, we still do not experience an individual being who is beyond the world. Nor are we able to adopt the secularized version of divine providence that the idea of progress assumes, with its emphasis on technical manipulation and control of our environment to serve human purposes. But what, then, do we experience? Is it only the void that remains as silent testimony to the absence of God? Or is it only the universe that remains after the demon of progress has been exorcized—a universe indifferent or even hostile to the human project, one that confronts us only with the prospect of increasing entropy and final extinction?

The answer to those questions is, in each case, yes. God is also the absence of God, the void. God is the universe even as hostile: God the enemy. The struggle of religious faith is to confront those faces of God and to realize, or return to, the God whom we may trust and to whom we may be committed.

In *Religion in the Making*, Alfred North Whitehead sums up our situation concisely: "Religion . . . is the transition from God the void to God the enemy, and from God the enemy to God the companion."[3] But our struggle is the more agonizing because we who had sensed the presence of God, who had worshiped the holy, who had joined in the communion of saints, are acutely aware of the absence, the indifference, even the hostility of the divine. Our transitions are, so to speak, in the wrong direction. From God the companion we have moved to God the enemy and perhaps from there to God the void.

This experience raises our anxieties, unsettles our sense of confidence, undermines our reliance on divine support. Yet in depriving us of assurance from a God who comforts us, the dis-ease of our situation is also salutary. We are pressed to acknowledge the extent to which our God has been too comfortable, too exclusively on a human scale. This downsizing of God has no doubt served special interests: the interests of men in legitimating deeply patriarchal social order and the interests of a rising bourgeoisie in glorifying upward mobility as of cosmic significance, to note two graphic instances. But God on a human scale has also provided comfort for those whose interests were not served: women and those left out of the boats rising with the tide of economic power.

Our experience of the loss of this comfortable God drives us not only to God the enemy and God the void but then also through them to reality still deeper and more inclusive. How we apprehend, construe, interpret, name this reality is far from trivial. The nominations are endless: Being, Being Itself, Suchness, Emptiness, Buddha-Nature, the Way, Lord, the One, the Holy Trinity, and many more. The ramifications of each alternative are complex and significant for the entire shape of a culture. So we cannot choose lightly among the alternatives. Nor can we convince ourselves that the choices do not matter, that all the alternatives are equally valid. And because there is no unassailable authority to which to appeal, we are faced with having to render judgments as to which alternatives are most adequate to the full range of our experience and shape that experience in ways that we affirm. Such judgments are enormously difficult. But they are also unavoidable if we are not to abdicate responsibility for orienting ourselves as we emerge from patriarchal images and concepts of God—as we move beyond God the Father.

Of the myriad alternatives even in only Christian traditions, I want to comment on two that I find compelling. I am persuaded that each of them focuses issues that need to be addressed in our situation after the collapse of belief in God as a being outside the world and the erosion of confidence in such substitutes for God as the idea of progress.

THE DIVINE AS INFINITE

The first designation that I find compelling is that of infinity. To affirm that the ultimate or the divine is infinite is to focus on the incomprehensible greatness of God. God is not bounded by any other reality. I do not believe that etymology is an infallible expositer of meaning. But in this case it guides us well. I mean "infinite" literally: not finite, not limited or bounded from the outside by any other entity. Rather, every reality whatsoever is in God, that ultimate reality in whom or within which we live and move and have our being. As infinite, God is not a being among other beings, nor a being outside the world. Such representations are endemic to the religious consciousness and may be not only unavoidable but in many contexts also beneficial. Yet the infinity of God precludes every final overagainstness, every boundedness from the outside.

We are, therefore, free from the literalism that takes forms of personal address and representations from our interpersonal experience to refer to God as one more entity. Instead, we may acknowledge and affirm that in our confessions of God we are characterizing the deepest and most inclusive reality that sustains us and of which we too are an expression.

This incomprehensible greatness of God means that the divine is not finally dependent on us. In denying this final dependence of the divine on the human, I do not mean what classical Christian theism affirmed as the absoluteness of God. That is, I do not mean the human has no effect on God, has no potential to contribute to the divine glory. Our human story does, I believe, participate in and therefore affect the divine life. But God is not confined to our history or dependent exclusively on our contributions to the realization of divine fulfillment.

In our era of the threat of nuclear annihilation and of dubious prospects for the viability of our ecosystem, this affirmation of the infinity of God is especially significant. Human life and the ecosystem of the planet earth are integral to the divine life and are therefore intrinsically valuable and valued. In contrast to the all too prevalent idolatry of the human in our culture, life on earth is not, however, itself of ultimate worth. To put it bluntly, God will survive our demise. This fact is not cause for complacency. The divine life will survive our demise as an ecosystem even as it incorporates our individual deaths. But in both cases, the loss is real. Accordingly, we are called to work together to preserve value wherever we can and to alleviate all avoidable suffering. Those challenges are massive and require our vigorous effort. Fervent as must be our engagement, we may, however, also celebrate the infinity of the divine which encompasses and sustains but also surpasses our individual and corporate existence.

To affirm the divine as infinite focuses not only on the greatness of God but also on the incomprehensibility of the divine. God is not bounded by any other reality; and God is also not limited by our ideas. This designation of God as infinite is, therefore, intrinsically critical in the sense that it rejects every attempt to confine God to human ideas of the divine. It is, in short, an idea that relativizes every claim to capture the ultimate or the absolute in our conceptions. As such, it is a powerful ally in our struggle to become free from the idolatrous literalism of traditions that constrain or oppress us.

GOD AS GOOD

Crucial as is the affirmation of the divine infinity, this affirmation alone is not enough. That God is incomprehensibly great is a necessary judgment against, and corrective to, our idolatry of the human—our tendency to downsize God, to reduce the divine to a human scale. But necessary as this affirmation is, it is not sufficient to elicit our trust and our commitment. God as infinite, as incomprehensibly great, in the words of the eleventh-century theologian Anselm of Canterbury, as that than which no greater can be conceived, attracts our wonder and awe.[4] Infinity alone does not, however, invite our faith.

Faith in the double sense of trust and commitment requires that God be not only great but also good. Here are raised our most fundamental religious questions: Is that deepest and most inclusive reality that we point to with the designation "infinite" also benevolent? Is the infinite more than an indifferent void? Is God the companion only a projection of our wishes even as God the enemy is a projection of our fears?

In responding to this array of questions—questions that pose the most fundamental challenges to faith—I turn to the central resources of Christian traditions. I am well aware that this procedure is circular, but I am also persuaded that the circularity is unavoidable. Christian images and ideas pervasively influence my awareness of, and fundamentally shape my approach to, such theological questions. The criticism and self-criticism entailed in the conception of the infinite are a needed corrective to the temptation to absolutize the images and ideas of particular traditions. But appropriately relativized and subject to self-criticism, particular images provide a concreteness that counters the utter abstractness or generality of a conception like the infinite. In a sense, the divine can and must also be scaled down to the human because faith depends on the power generated through such particularity. The divine is all too easily subject to domestication—which is what abstract or general conceptions like infinity counter. But God may also be eviscerated, which is what more concrete or particular images must resist.

For me, the goodness of the divine is mediated through the image of God incarnate: spirit embodied. This image is not alien to or incompatible with the conception of the infinite. Indeed, it is the necessary correlate of that conception. The human cannot finally stand over against the divine, as another reality limiting the infinite. Nor is there a final opposition between body and spirit. Indeed, even evil cannot finally be excluded from the infinite. But in the image of God incarnate is expressed the divine bearing and trans-formation of evil in all its particularity. Spirit is embodied; the infinite is incarnate. As Athanasius put it succinctly in the fourth century, "God became human so that we might be made divine."[5]

Only this embodied spirit elicits trust and commitment. Those of us who are Christians affirm this spirit as embodied in Jesus; and we experience this spirit embodied in communities that share trust in and commitment to the commonwealth of God, that deepest and most inclusive community for which we are destined. Christian churches have as their reason for being their intention to serve as an institutional expression of this inclusive community. In this sense, churches may indeed be a continuation of the incarnation, an embodiment on earth of the holy spirit, the commonwealth of God, that inclusive and transforming community in which there is neither Jew nor Greek, slave nor free, male nor female.

Our experience of this inclusive and transforming community is not—even for those of us who call ourselves Christians—confined to particular Christian churches. Nor is this experience altogether discontinuous with the testimony of other religious traditions. Even when there are quite basic differences in orientation, there may still be significant shared concerns. To take a central example, the emphasis in Hindu, Buddhist, and Taoist traditions on overcoming our self-preoccupations through recognition of our final union with the ultimate has very substantial common ground with the expe-rience of self-transcendence in community. Yet despite my deep attraction to other alternatives and to analogues in other traditions, I am well aware that my own affirmation of spirit embodied in inclusive and transforming community is directly continuous with Christian traditions.

The continuities extend even to the central concerns expressed in the conception of God as a being outside the world and in the attempt to substitute progress for the divine. The infinite as em-bodied spirit is not a being conceived as one more entity and rep-resented as over against the world. But the infinite as embodied spirit is also not less than personal. We experience this reality of the divine in the communities we share with others. In those communities, we aspire to be inspirited, to be delivered from our own self-preoccupations into a finally all-inclusive commonwealth that we affirm as divine. In this aspiration, we therefore also testify to our inheritance, if not from the idea of progress, then certainly from the affirmation of divine providence that it secularized. We too affirm a hope that is emphatically not yet realized. We trust in a reality to whose emergence we are committed.

To hold firm this trust and this commitment is the struggle of faith. It is a struggle not only to affirm but to contribute to the realization of God or the commonwealth of God. To participate in this struggle is to move from the recognition of God the void to fighting against God the enemy to collaboration with God the companion. This movement toward transforming and inclusive community is the reality we experience and may name as divine. This emerging community, this process of transformation and inclusion, is the divine reality beyond God the Father: the commonwealth of God, the divine-human body, the holy spirit into which we may be incorporated.

——— 3

Christology in the Context of Pluralism

To identify God with movement toward transforming and inclusive community poses a special challenge for religious commitment. To put it bluntly, religious communities have tended much more to hold exclusivistic positions than to foster inclusiveness. This tendency is certainly evident in Christian theology and especially in claims for the uniqueness of Christ. For that reason, a consideration of Christology in the context of religious pluralism offers an apt case study of the relationship between particular commitment and inclusive community.

In the opening section of his *Institutes of the Christian Religion*, John Calvin registers an organizing principle for his theology: "Nearly all wisdom we possess, that is to say, true and sound wisdom, consists of two parts: the knowledge of God and of ourselves."[1] This correlation of our knowledge of God and of ourselves has shaped much of Reformed theology since the time of Calvin. But it is also an apt characterization of the structure of theological reflection across the spectrum of Christian confessions. The reason is christological: for Christians, conceptions of God and the self are correlative because our reflections on the divine and the human are focused in the figure of Jesus Christ.

Insofar as Christian reflection on the divine and the human is christologically focused, it may seem irreducibly particular. But this view overlooks the fact that the relationship between the figure of Jesus Christ on the one hand and conceptions of God and the self on the other allows movement in both directions. Accordingly, every Christology is explicitly or at least implicitly also a theology and an anthropology. As a result, while christological motifs interpret and express particular Christian traditions, they at the same time offer points of contact with the conceptions of the human and the ultimate developed in other traditions.[2]

This dialectical relationship between interpretations of the figure of Jesus Christ and our conceptions of God and the self suggests a three-step approach to the topic of Christology in the context of religious pluralism: first, to explore the impact of christological motifs on our awareness of ourselves; then, to illustrate the diverse interpretations of the relationship of the human to the divine that have emerged in Christian history and that continue to characterize our own time; and, finally, to consider similarities and differences between those understandings and views of the self and the ultimate articulated in other religious traditions.

IMAGES OF CHRIST AND CHRISTIAN SELF-AWARENESS

In art, liturgy, ethical precept, and theological interpretation, the figure of Jesus Christ embodies a double awareness in our consciousness as Christians. In being confronted with that figure, we experience both grace and judgment. In the classic theological formula, we apprehend ourselves as *simul justus et peccator*—at once justified and sinner.

In the figure of Jesus, we see ourselves judged in our hostility, our insecurity, our ignorance, our fear. This judgment is almost overwhelmingly acute when we face Jesus on the cross. Over and over again we hear in the biblical accounts and their echoes throughout Christian traditions that he hangs there on the cross because of us. We opposed him because he threatened our prerogatives. We allowed those insecure in their authority to play on our ignorance as we joined the cry to crucify him. Even those few of us who tried to follow him in the end betrayed him in our uncertainty and fear.

Nor is this sense of judgment reflected only in the accounts of the crucifixion. It pervades the biblical narratives which lead inexorably to the cross. In these narratives, as in our own experience, we all too often are the ones who demean and criticize others. We are the ones who pronounce judgment and thereby stand with the Pharisees and scribes over against the publicans and sinners. We look on and grumble about those who fail to meet our standards. We compare ourselves favorably to those who know they fall short. So we become those who mistakenly think we need no healing. Because we are satisfied with what we have, we choose to play it safe with our talents. In our self-righteousness, we are not the ones who go away justified before God. Instead, in story after story and incident after incident, if we look and listen at all, we can only see and hear ourselves judged.

And yet somehow judgment is not the only or the last word. Even as we experience our responsibility—our guilt—in confronting the figure of the innocent victim on the cross, we also sense the attraction of that figure. Throughout the history of Christian thought and devotion, countless metaphors and analogies and even theories of atonement have sought to capture this sense of a movement beyond our guilt. The least elaborate phrase from biblical traditions on is the simple affirmation that he died for us. In that suffering death, we see the fullest, the most extreme, expression of love he lived among us. And that love—which, following Jesus, we call divine—that divine love pursues all of us humans, even the least of us, even us here and now.

In this respect also, the cross etches in starkest form the truth that Jesus is portrayed as teaching and living throughout his ministry. Outcasts and tax collectors like Levi and Zacchaeus are called to join him, as are women reputed to be prostitutes like Mary Magdalene. The lost coin and the lost sheep are sought and found, to great rejoicing. The prodigal son is welcomed home with open arms. The laborers in the vineyard who worked only one hour are not distinguished from the others. People are rounded up in the streets to join the feast. The kingdom or rule or commonwealth of God is breaking in. It is open to all of us who do not close ourselves off in our own self-satisfaction. Indeed, it is a dynamic love that reaches out and includes all who are excluded from other communities. It brings into the divine love feast with the world all who have been kept on the outside.

So we, like our forebears in the first century, are proffered an invitation to which we respond in one way or another. The invitation is extended. Membership is open in the kingdom or commonwealth of God—in the divine-human body that is the holy spirit. But many of us, like almost all the contemporaries of Jesus, see that open invitation more as a threat than a promise. The open invitation makes no allowances for differential qualifications. The spendthrift young son is treated as well as the responsible older brother. Those who work only an hour in the vineyard receive no less than those who toiled all day. The temptation to resentment and self-righteousness is difficult to resist.

To succumb to this temptation was the response of those of us who opposed Jesus in the first century; and it continues to be a standard response among us today. This response turns the promise of God into a threat to our security, our self-esteem, our self-satisfaction. As a result, it closes the open door to the feast of God. But in limiting the invitation, we exclude ourselves, not others. We who presume to be on the inside in the end find ourselves outside complaining about the lack of qualifications in those who are included.

To live out of our awareness of ourselves as *simul justus et peccator*—at once justified and sinner—is, then, an ongoing challenge. In the love Jesus lived among us and expressed in his death at our hands, we are affirmed in our very unworthiness. The assurance that forgiveness and healing are offered allows us to own our neediness. We are delivered from the temptation to defensive self-righteousness that attacks others to avoid acknowledging our own sense of unworthiness. At the same time, we can identify with the whole creation in its brokenness and neediness. In this identification we are enabled in turn to accept and love others as we move toward the inclusive community that Jesus pointed to in speaking of the kingdom of God.

ILLUSTRATIONS FROM CHRISTIAN TRADITIONS

To our ears, talk about the kingdom of God has a ring to it that is both familiar and at the same time somehow quaint. After all, kingship of a substantive sort—royalty that actually rules—is decidedly anachronistic in our times. And our contemporaries seem less and less to speak of or to the divine. So even though the phrase "kingdom of God" has a comfortably and comfortingly familiar sound, it does not directly and unambiguously express effective power impinging on us here and now.

But just this divine power in our midst is what talk about the kingdom of God expresses in the biblical accounts of the ministry of Jesus. God is not a deity ruling from afar. Nor is the divine domesticated in the worship of the temple. Instead, the kingdom of God is imminent, breaking in on every side, even already in our midst. This divine rule or power is again and again depicted as utterly at odds with our ordinary expectations, as shattering the familiar and the comfortable, as inaugurating a new aeon in which established patterns are reversed.

There is an apocalyptic strain through much of this New Testament language, a strain that stresses the tension with the old and the imminent breaking in of the transforming power of the new. The new age stands utterly over against this fallen time and calls forth judgment on it. And yet the radically new is not distant or alien. Rather, the God who was thought to be afar off has come near and is in the midst of the human right here. The future age is dawning right now.

In the classic formulations of orthodoxy, the Christian church resisted attempts to separate God from creation. Scandalous though it was to Greek sensibilities, the Council of Nicea affirmed that God was indeed directly implicated in the created order: the Christ who dwelled among us was God of God, Light of Light, very God of very God, begotten, not made, of one substance with the divine.[3] God was not utterly transcendent and related to the world only at one remove through the Christ. Instead, God was affirmed to be directly and intimately involved with the created order even in its fallenness, to be incarnate even in human flesh.

In and through the occasionally unseemly political and ecclesiastical machinations that surrounded the Council of Nicea, this affirmation of God as directly and intimately involved with creation became a standard of orthodoxy. But we all know that standards of orthodoxy are thought to be necessary only when there are live alternatives attracting interest and commitment. Consequently, we are not surprised that there were attractive competing positions in the fourth and fifth centuries—positions that can plausibly trace their lineage back to the Bible and that also certainly continue to have progeny in our own time.

Probably the most potent and persistent of the alternatives in the history of Christian piety is the very one that the orthodox formulas of Nicea opposed. This alternative is common to all those positions so emphasizing the otherness of the divine that ordinary human life is utterly divorced from its ultimate destiny. God is affirmed as absolutely transcendent; and the aim of faith is salvation understood as deliverance from earthly trials to the beatific vision of God or to a heavenly existence completely discontinuous with life on earth.

In the first centuries of Christian history, the theological controversies that eventuated in the Nicean formulations provide one illustration of this preoccupation with the proper conception of the relationship of the ultimate to the earthly. Another extended illustration is the powerful ferment encompassed in the rubric of Gnosticism. In its many variations, Gnosticism expressed an otherworldly orientation that both elicited opposition and attracted followers in Christian communities. In and through their elaborate cosmologies and Christologies, Gnostics agreed in envisioning salvation as the liberation of the spiritual element of the human. In gnostic anthropology and soteriology, this spiritual element is located in the souls of certain select individuals and its salvation entails deliverance from the lower constituents of the human, not only from the carnal or material body but also from the soul. Such complete deliverance from this life is required because the spiritual element is a total stranger imprisoned in the intrinsically evil world of matter.

Early theologians like Irenaeus, Tertullian, and Hippolytus and their successors through the centuries have resisted the influence of such gnostic motifs in Christian thought and practice. But the pattern represented in even the most extreme gnostic formulations is still a recurrent one in Christian piety. The believer is a stranger in an utterly fallen world; and salvation is release from this world— often through correct acknowledgment of the truths of faith—for existence in heaven with God.

This representation of salvation as individual existence in heaven is not, of course, the only pattern in Christian piety. Nor are the various patterns mutually exclusive. In medieval piety, for example, confidence in a heavenly destiny for the faithful continued as a significant theme. But the affirmation of the incarnation—of the enfleshment of the ultimate, the human embodiment of God—also authorized very concrete and specific interest in the location of divine power in this world. This emphatic interest in the particularity of incarnation informs and structures quite diverse expressions of medieval piety: enthusiastic attraction to miracles as sensible evidence of the irruption of the activity of God into particular human beings or places or objects worthy of veneration; excitement about pilgrimages, especially to the Holy Land; even the attention of theologians to carefully defining exactly how the divine is present in the material form of the eucharistic elements, how the body and blood of the Christ are present in the bread and wine of the mass.[4]

PATTERNS IN CONTEMPORARY COMMITMENT

The great diversity in medieval piety illustrates the multiplicity of patterns of Christian reflection and action in even a nominally unified period. Similarly, in our own time multiple patterns that have dominated Christian traditions continue to be very much in evidence. In particular, the representation of the goal of life as individual salvation in a heavenly or divine realm sharply contrasted to earthly existence in space and time continues to exercise a powerful hold on the religious imagination. But less traditional interpretations of humanity in relation to the ultimate conditions of human existence have become increasingly prevalent as well.

Such less traditional interpretations are continuous with patterns of the past. To note those continuities illuminates both the historical sources and the contemporary power of positions that in other respects are quite diverse. But despite undeniable continuities, there are also striking and significant shifts in interpretation. We see both the continuities and the systematic shifts if we look at contemporary variations on the themes of gnostic otherworldliness and medieval incarnationalism.

In the case of the gnostic pattern, definite continuities are evident in many of the forms of modern individualism. The true self is defined in sharp contrast to ordinary people. This true self is a project to be achieved, not a historical given. Consequently, individuals must become free from their bondage to personal ties, social roles, and cultural expectations. Precisely in this liberation from the ordinary, the authentic person attains to self-conscious identity and individuality.

But despite this continuity in emphasis on the imperative to free the truly human from its imprisonment in the mundane, there is a decisive shift in many contemporary adaptations of this gnostic pattern. The shift has to do with the ultimate goal or context for the human. That shift is most stark or dramatic in the explicitly atheistic forms of modern existentialism. In this case, the individual is portrayed as struggling in a hostile or at best indifferent universe to create whatever meaning or value is attainable. Thus atheistic existentialism affirms the highly individualistic conception of the self developed as the human correlate of an utterly transcendent heaven or God while at the same time repudiating as misguided or at least outdated every belief in the existence of such an ultimate.

Contemporary Christian theology and piety only infrequently identify with this existentialist denial of the existence of God— although there are major post-Enlightenment theologians who have argued that the divine is not a being and that, therefore, to speak of the existence of God is conceptually indefensible. But even apart from this contention, post-Enlightenment theology and piety still exemplify a decisive shift from the gnostic pattern. In post-Enlightenment Christian commitment as in atheistic existentialism, there are powerful currents that run counter to the otherworldly tendencies of much traditional piety. In contrast to the gnostic motif of spiritual escape from matter and its counterpart in Christian piety of individual salvation in heaven, these currents are programmatically this-worldly in orientation even when they are highly individualistic. Consequently, the goal of the religious life becomes authenticity here and now in response to an ever-present divine invitation or obedience in this life to the call of God to faithful discipleship. Thus the gnostic pattern continues to be evident in a strongly individualistic emphasis, but its characteristic otherworldliness with reference to either a heavenly realm or the divine is strikingly absent.

Like the gnostic pattern, the orientation of medieval incarnationalism also continues to be represented even as it is very significantly changed. The insistence in the incarnational pattern that divine power is effective in this world is also present in much contemporary Christian commitment. But along with continuity in this commitment, there is a very significant shift in the location of the divine power.

The fate of the category of miracle in the modern period may serve to epitomize the change. While for medieval piety the category of miracle referred to specific sensible evidence of the activity of God in particular persons or places or objects, for contemporary faith the term more characteristically has far greater generality of reference. God is affirmed as the sustaining power of the universe and is praised for the beauty, regularity, and dependability of the cosmos. Even the most secular of our contemporaries may be heard to exclaim, "Why, it's a miracle!" But whether secular or religious, fewer and fewer of us insist that a sense of wonder at the marvelous and unexpected outcome of a situation requires belief in a special irruption of the activity of God into the natural order of the universe. Instead, if the sustaining and providential activity of God is affirmed, it is construed as operative in and through natural regularities. In this instance, too, there is a pronounced shift away from the traditional pattern of central concern with an otherworldly realm or being. But in contrast to the tendency of existentialism and its Christian counterparts, the pattern in this case emphasizes inclusion and sustenance rather than individual identity over against an alien world.

In effect, contemporary variations on the themes of gnostic otherworldliness and medieval incarnationalism illustrate two different approaches to appropriating Christian commitments in the face of the collapse for many people of more traditional representations of the goal of life as salvation in a heavenly or divine realm set over against earthly existence. Each approach continues definite motifs or tendencies from those more traditional representations. In its strongly individualistic orientation and its emphasis on defining the self over against a sharply delineated other, contemporary adaptations of the gnostic pattern continue what have become characteristically Protestant tendencies. Similarly, in strongly affirming the presence of the ultimate in even physical life, adaptations of the incarnational pattern exemplify the sacramental motifs most fully expressed in Orthodox and Roman Catholic traditions.

Despite this significant difference in historical antecedents and in the dominant emphasis of contemporary formulations, the two approaches nonetheless have much in common precisely because both are attempts to appropriate Christian commitments without orienting life to the goal of salvation in a heavenly or divine realm set over against earthly existence. Viewed as responses to the same challenge—namely, the collapse of this traditional religious orientation—the opposed tendencies of the two approaches may be seen to be complementary. The incarnational motif contributes an appreciation of every point and moment of ordinary life as embodying the ultimate and exhibiting the divine glory here and now. Standing in potentially complementary tension with this affirmation are contemporary variants of the gnostic pattern, which resist every unqualified domestication of the divine but also avoid a retreat into otherworldliness.

Positions seeking to actualize this potential complementarity aim at a fusion of motifs not unlike the marriage of apocalyptic and incarnational themes in the early church. The God who was thought to be afar off has come near and is here among us. The future age is dawning right now. And yet God is not completely at home in our world. Instead, God is also the utter otherness that calls and challenges us in our provincialism and self-righteousness, that unsettles us from our comfortable exclusions of others, that moves us toward the all-inclusive community that alone embodies and expresses the divine, the holy spirit.

THE SELF IN RELATION TO THE ULTIMATE ACROSS TRADITIONS

As I noted in chapter 1, traditional Christianity is not alone in its orientation toward salvation in another realm. Also in other religious communities, among the most potent and persistent of tendencies, especially in popular piety, is an emphasis on the otherness of the ultimate and a correlative understanding of the goal of the religious life as deliverance from the deficiencies endemic to earthly existence. In sum, orientation to a transcendent realm pictured as starkly over against this world is prevalent in an impressive range of religious traditions.

To emphasize the significance of this otherworldly orientation, I again note its prevalence across religious traditions for at least two thousand years. In Hindu theology and piety, there is a pervasive concern with attaining release (*moksha*) from the recurrent cycle of birth and death (*samsara*) that defines historical life. Despite radical criticism of the prevailing Hindu views on such issues as the status of the self, the dominant tendency in Theravada Buddhism is similarly an orientation toward attaining freedom from *samsara*. In Mahayana Buddhism, the pattern is more complex both because of the contention that the goal of life or the ultimate (*nirvana*) and ordinary historical existence (*samsara*) are one and the same and because of Taoist and other East Asian influences. But there are still widespread and influential Mahayana Buddhist interpretations of the goal of the religious life as deliverance from this defiled world through rebirth in a pure land or the Western paradise, to use imagery common to the numerous schools of Japanese Pure Land Buddhism.

Even in traditions with strong reasons for resisting this tendency, interpretations of the goal of the religious life as deliverance from earthly existence emerge again and again. For example, in the case of Islam, despite a thoroughgoing concern to shape the whole of the life of Muslim communities, there is nonetheless a pervasive emphasis on this life as only the preparation for an eternal destiny in heaven or hell. Or in the case of Taoism, a programmatic philosophical rejection of every form of dualism still allows and even encourages a popular preoccupation with immortality as a transformed although still physical existence in one or another paradise.

This concern for attaining salvation in another realm is, of course, no more the only or exclusive pattern in other religious traditions than it is in Christianity. Indeed, in a number of other traditions, this otherworldly orientation is self-consciously juxtaposed or even opposed to a quite different pattern. In general terms, this alternative pattern is a mystically attained and/or philosophically argued monism in which the self and the ultimate are in intimate communion or even completely merged into an undifferentiated unity. Vedantic Hinduism, Zen Buddhism, Taoist wisdom, and some forms of Sufi mysticism exemplify this pattern. In each case, the apparent dualism of popular piety directed toward salvation or release from this life is vigorously resisted. Instead, the whole of reality is suffused with or construed as integral to the ultimate.

At first glance, this alternative pattern seems to break fundamentally with the otherworldly tendency also evident in the same traditions. But on closer review, this initial impression is misleading. In actuality, each instance of the monistic pattern also represents a certain disengagement from the exigencies of this life. The disengagement is most dramatic in the Vedantic Hindu relegation of phenomenal life to the status of illusion (*maya*). But it is evident in less dramatic forms as well. In the attainment of the Taoist sage or the Sufi mystic, there is a distancing of the self from ordinary historical life. And even in and through the insistence of Zen that the enlightened one returns to the marketplace, insight offers deliverance from entanglements in that arena. In short, orientation to a single unified reality need not entail engagement with the concerns of ordinary historical life.

Yet despite the patterns of preoccupation with attaining release from this world on the one hand and mystical or philosophical orientation to an undifferentiated whole of reality on the other, the same traditions also have resources for decisively shaping this historical life in its particularity. Hindu traditions structure Indian existence in its entirety and celebrate contributions from all stations and stages of life. In its insistence that ultimate reality is precisely this historical realm, Buddhist insight not only offers deliverance from worldly entanglements but also attains the vision to behold the ultimate in every detail of lived experience. Similarly, the Taoist sense of unity with the natural order in turn shapes every human activity. In the case of Islam, otherworldly expectations and mystic rapture still allow powerful affirmation of the religious significance of ordering the corporate life of the obedient community here and now.

Such resources from the Hindu, Buddhist, Taoist, and Islamic communities are further enriched from traditions like Judaism and Confucianism, which have characteristically had a strongly ethical and this-worldly orientation. The prophetic strain in Jewish traditions with its emphasis on living out the covenant with God in concrete social forms is impressive in this connection. So too is the Confucian insistence that the way of heaven is intrinsically concerned with proper, respectful, and harmonious relations among human beings.

The double challenge confronting all these traditions is precisely the one also facing Christian faith today. It is to repudiate every form of Gnosticism and to affirm this world—not just this or that miracle, as in medieval piety, but this world as a whole for what it can be—while at the same time maintaining a sense of profound tension between the ultimate that is emerging and the actual as it is. The challenge is, in short, to live out the union of incarnation and apocalyptic.

Each of the various religious traditions offers ample illustration of family resemblances to the two partners of this union. In a general sense, all of the instances of emphasis on the disjunction between this world and the ultimate exemplify the tension that characterizes the apocalyptic motif. As for the incarnational motif, the situation is more complex because central Christian traditions—orthodox christological formulations and medieval piety, to note the two instances already discussed—resist generalization of a category that is construed as irreducibly particular. But insofar as the conception of incarnation is taken to refer to the fundamental affirmation that the ultimate is intimately involved with the world, this motif is present across an impressive range of traditions both in representations of an order that God creates and redeems and also in holistic ontologies that include all of reality in the ultimate.

Because the various religious traditions offer instances of the apocalyptic and incarnational motifs in this generalized sense, they also provide the resources for developing an integrated position that unites the two tendencies. This position maintains a continuing tension between affirmation of the ultimate in this world on the one hand and criticism directed toward reshaping historical life on the other. The result is not only to affirm this world in general but also to stand critically over against all those specific institutional forces that resist the realization of the ultimate in concrete historical forms.

The critical dimension of positions that express both the apocalyptic and the incarnational motifs is not infrequently directed against religious ideas and institutions. Indeed, the tendencies opposed are the prevailing ones across religious traditions: an otherworldly orientation that disengages from historical life; piety that seeks the irruption of the divine only in this or that arbitrary event or individual; apprehension of reality as a single undifferentiated unity, which in effect legitimates every extant historical arrangement; and interpretation of religious symbolism so as to reinforce the provincialism and self-righteousness that exclude others. But this resistance within religious communities to views prevalent across traditions is in turn significant for the patterns of collaboration among those communities.

This collaboration typically does not attend directly to opposed tendencies either among the traditions or within each of them.

Instead, such collaboration focuses on an issue or concern that is a shared one despite differences in orientation and commitment. Global threats like nuclear war or world hunger are the most dramatic instances of issues that elicit shared concern and allow a common stance across religious traditions. But even when collaboration on such global issues deliberately avoids consideration of differences within and among traditions, its stance is often one of criticism over against the broader society. Thus the development of common positions on global issues in effect participates in resisting the tendencies across religious traditions toward other-worldliness and the uncritical legitimation of existing historical arrangements. Put positively, such collaboration expresses the development of this-worldly and critical tendencies across religious traditions. It is eloquent if often silent testimony to the marriage of the apocalyptic and incarnational motifs.

This marriage of apocalyptic and incarnational motifs in a variety of traditions is certainly significant for a consideration of Christology in the context of religious pluralism. It indicates that in other traditions, too, the ultimate may be apprehended as intimately involved with but not completely at home in this world, as integrally united with the human, even, or especially, in its suffering action toward a finally all-inclusive community. This shared apprehension of the human and the ultimate constitutes substantial common ground from which to resist the socially uncritical and otherworldly tendencies prevalent in both Christian and other religious traditions. Thus for this approach to Christology, the context of religious pluralism offers not only a host of new positions but also the prospect of allies in other traditions who share a common commitment to inclusive community.

Theology and the Comparative History of Religions

The prospect of increasing collaboration among adherents of different religious traditions as they engage common issues has its counterpart in what I take to be a very significant development in the study of religion: renewed convergence between the history of religions and theology.[1] This convergence is not simply an intriguing intellectual development in the taxonomy of academic disciplines. It is rather the expression of a powerful historical movement that compels our attention. To elaborate and defend this contention, I will first outline the underlying historical development, then discuss its implications for both the history of religions and theology, and finally sketch an approach to religious thought or theology that is viable in this emerging situation.

THE RELIGIOUS HISTORY OF HUMANKIND

The historical development that informs the renewed convergence of study in the history of religions and theology is the increasingly widespread awareness of the unity of the religious history of humankind.[2] It is certainly not a new development that the history of the various ostensibly discrete religious communities may be construed as parts of a larger whole. But neither this unity nor its significance—including its theological significance—has been as clearly recognized in the past.

Similarly, it is not a new development that members of one religious community in effect contribute to the evolution of another

tradition. Think of the massive instances of cross-tradition influences in the past: the medieval trilogue among Jews, Christians,
and Muslims or of all of them with the thought of Aristotle; the
commingling of the "three teachings"—Confucian, Buddhist, and
Taoist—in China; and the role that the nineteenth-century Christian
missionary movement in Asia played in the religious development
of the non-Christian world. But our contemporary situation is nonetheless different insofar as increasing numbers of people, often
over great distances, in effect participate at the same time in their
own tradition and in others through their observations, study, and
even religious discipline. The shift is from a time of being involved
without realizing it in the ongoing process of development of a
neighboring community to a dawning era of self-conscious engagement in that process.

An example or two may help to make this abstract assertion more
concrete. Christian missionaries in Asia in the last century had an
enormous impact. Part of the impact was through the conversion
of individual Indians or Japanese or Africans to Christianity. But
at least as significant and in the long run almost certainly more
influential has been the effect of Christian missionaries on the
indigenous traditions with which they came in contact. Even
though they held formal membership only in Christian churches,
missionaries also participated in the ongoing development of those
other traditions as they encountered the onslaught of the modern
West. Today we are more aware of those multiple levels of participation. As a result, missionaries are less likely to view their role
exclusively as converting individuals to Christianity and are more
open to both learning from other traditions and contributing to
their ongoing development.

Certainly this interaction among traditions is not confined to
contact between different religious communities. It is also evident
in interactions within a nominally unified religious tradition. Consider the difference in attitude between a Lutheran who has never
been close to Christians other than Lutherans and a Lutheran who
has as his or her best friend a Catholic or a Baptist. Fewer and
fewer of us grow up in a situation where we are not close to people
in communities different from our own. Maybe they are all Baptists,
but not all fundamentalist Baptists. More likely, our friends and
neighbors include not only Christians of several denominations

and confessions but also Jews—and, increasingly, Buddhists, Hindus, and Muslims as well. As a result, we participate in however limited a way also in those other communities, which in turn affects how we see not only them but also ourselves.

As more of us become more aware of our participation in multiple traditions, we in effect see both our own traditions and the traditions of other communities from a comparative perspective. This comparative perspective is both more informed and more self-critical. The result is that our knowledge of ourselves may become more and more like the knowledge that others have of us. At the same time, at least when we are at our best, we aspire to knowledge of others that approximates their own knowledge of themselves.

As this formulation suggests, in this situation there is more and more common ground in the fields of theology and history of religions. Indeed, insofar as this complex historical transition to an increasingly widespread sense of critical and self-critical participation in multiple developing traditions is the context for contemporary understandings and expressions of religious communities, sharp distinctions between theology and the history of religions become less and less tenable. This development has definite implications for both theology and the history of religions.

THE HISTORY OF RELIGIONS
AND THEOLOGY

It is worth noting how recent and uncharacteristic in human history is a clear differentiation between theology and the history of religions. In the West before the Enlightenment and throughout the histories of virtually all other traditions, theologians or those in similar positions of intellectual responsibility in other religious traditions were presumed to have such knowledge as was available or desirable concerning what has come to be understood as the history of religions. That there should be a separate scholarly guild to provide information about other religious traditions is an innovation of the Enlightenment in the West. Even more recent is the intention that this information should be objective as distinguished from either serving the apologetic purposes of a religious community or debunking the pretentions of one tradition through unfavorable comparison to another.

Despite its relatively brief duration, a clear differentiation of the history of religions from theology has been enormously productive. The aim of accurately and systematically describing the religious traditions of others in principle apart from both apologetic and iconoclastic interests has contributed immeasurably to the philological and historical understanding of the data of religious history. Indeed, this study has often been in the forefront of cross-cultural understanding as Western universities have only gradually moved out of very provincial conceptions—especially of the humanities. Missionary concerns and other forms of religious or antireligious motivation no doubt provided much of the energy for this study. But the development of a discipline in principle differentiated from the theological or ideological interests of any one community has supported and accelerated the remarkable collection of data in the history of religions from the Enlightenment on and especially in the last century and a half.

To note and applaud a contemporary convergence of study in the history of religions and theology need not and should not entail any interest in simply reversing the very productive differentiation of the two in the recent history of Western universities. But the contemporary context of increasing awareness of interconnections across religious traditions does provide the opportunity to consider again the relations between theology and the history of religions. In particular, the recognition of greater common ground in the two fields allows a moving beyond the mutual stereotypes that have become inaccurate and counterproductive.

The mutual stereotypes have arisen in the first instance because of the concern on the part of the history of religions to differentiate itself from theology. The result has been a self-characterization of the history of religions as objective study of other traditions in their own right rather than for apologetic purposes. In this self-characterization is the implied and not infrequently also explicit contrast to the traditional theological disciplines, which are suspect insofar as they combine the historical description of data with concern for the normative commitments of a particular religious community. In its sharpest form the contrast is, in short, between objective and value-free study on the one hand and ideologically determined apologetics on the other.

This self-characterization of the history of religions has been influential in providing academic legitimation for the study of religion, especially in American colleges and universities—a process of legitimation that is not without its ironies. Faculty members and departments have argued for the academic respectability of their efforts on the basis of philological and historical rigor and objectivity in contributing to understanding both other cultures and earlier periods of Western traditions. At the same time, the greatest interest of students—and of many faculty members as well—has been in offerings that relate such studies to current issues of personal values and public policy. Thus even when the emphasis on the objectivity of the study of religion has been most pronounced, concern with normative questions has been considerable.

This apparently irrepressible interest in normative questions is not, of course, confined to the study of religion. But the recurrent expression of such concerns provides the opportunity to criticize the conception of academic study as value-free inquiry—instead of appealing to that very conception in attempting to secure respectability for the study of religion. Put positively, the study of religion should aspire to become a model of responsible attention to normative questions, especially because such questions have received insufficient careful study in the modern secular university.

In the context of increasing awareness across religious traditions, normative questions become all the more salient. Historical study of developing traditions that interact with one's own almost unavoidably raises comparative questions about relative adequacy to an increasingly shared experience. The process works in both directions: appraisal is directed toward what is observed and also reflected back on the values of the observer. As a result, both our awareness of others and our self-understandings increasingly focus on the question of truth from a critical and a comparative perspective.

There is, to be sure, the amply illustrated limiting case of investigators who insist that they are only describing what they see and that they are interested neither in assessing it nor in allowing it to impinge on their own views. This orientation has contributed extensively to the accumulation of data about other traditions and in this regard is worthy of respect. But the stated intention of this approach, to understand another tradition on its own terms, has the effect of refusal to entertain even the possibility of its truth. Of course, the further result is that the adequacy of the investigator's own views is simply presumed. Ironically, this uncritical stance toward one's own values and disinterest in the normative claims of others is not altogether unlike the position of theologians who want only to commend their own views in comparison to the commitments of others.

To participate self-consciously and self-critically in two or more traditions as parts of a more inclusive whole is, then, a rejection of every such presumed adequacy of one's own views. For the historian of religions—and certainly for the comparative historian of religions—the result is that study becomes fully cross-cultural as inquiry directed toward understanding the other also invites reexamination of one's own traditions. Similarly, for the theologian, exposition and advocacy of his or her own position cannot proceed on the basis of authorities simply presumed to be incommensurate with those of other communities and inaccessible to participants in other traditions. Instead, in this case, too, understanding other traditions and representing one's own are intimately involved with each other because they are directed toward only provisionally separate streams of an increasingly shared history.

This situation of increasing awareness across traditions poses a fundamental challenge to the whole enterprise of theology. In this sense, the situation of theology is different from that of the history of religions. Even if historians of religions cannot uncritically presume their own values, they do not have the professional responsibility to represent the position of a particular tradition. But theologians and those in analogous positions in nontheistic traditions at least in the past typically have had precisely this responsibility: to represent the traditions of a particular community so as to interpret and in turn also to shape the experience of its members. How is this responsibility of the theologian to be executed in the context of an emerging world culture in which participants in any one tradition also increasingly participate self-consciously in the religious life of humanity as a whole?

RELIGIOUS THOUGHT AS COMPARATIVE AND CONSTRUCTIVE

At least in its monotheistic forms, theology has always been grounded in particular traditions and from that base has sought to understand what is universally true. The foundation in particularity and the universality of reference continue to be definitive of the enterprise properly construed. But both terms of this polarity also assume a distinctive character in the context of an emerging world culture.

The images, the ideas, the norms and injunctions, the ritual and institutional patterns that constitute the traditions of his or her particular community decisively shape the experience that the theologian interprets. But as theologians and their counterparts in nontheistic traditions become increasingly aware of religious and ideological communities other than their own, they also are at least indirectly and peripherally influenced by those other communities. Consequently, they participate in multiple traditions even when they affirm their own community as fundamental to their particular identity.

A similar insinuation of multiplicity or plurality characterizes the universality of reference of theology. The aim of the undertaking is still to seek to understand the ultimate conditions of human life, to interpret the whole of experience in its most encompassing context. Included in that whole of experience are, however, an imposing array of alternative symbolizations of the ultimate conditions or the most encompassing context of human life. Even such almost completely formal terms as "the ultimate" and "the whole" entail elaborate traditions of assumptions and implications. So, too, of course, do more particular terms—"God" or *sunyata*, for example. In sum, in the context of increased awareness across traditions, even to formulate the universalistic intention of theology and its analogues in nontheistic traditions already unavoidably involves a comparative dimension.

The novelty of the contemporary situation should not be overstated. After all, awareness of differences among religious traditions on virtually every issue, including the question of how the ultimate is most appropriately conceived or addressed or realized, is scarcely an unprecedented development. Within nominally unified communities, there have always been controversies among competing alternative interpretations of shared traditions. Similarly, conflict between clearly distinguished communities has been only too characteristic of the religious landscape over the centuries. But what is new is the increasingly widespread recognition both of substantial change over time within continuing communities and of systematic parallels in the development of traditions that are historically only remotely related.

Both change within a continuing community and apparent similarities across distinct communities allow traditionalist interpretations. Change over time is in this case construed as a series of heretical deviations from what can be identified and must be affirmed as the strictly maintained standard of orthodoxy. Similarly, the impression of parallels in quite different traditions is resisted because it is held to result from a comparison of positions that are, when rightly viewed, incommensurable. In the case of such traditionalist interpretations, increased awareness of both change within and parallels between religious communities is resisted and in turn countered through reiterated appeals to an inerrant authority that guarantees unique truth.

This assertion of traditional authority continues to exercise impressive and at times volatile power, perhaps especially in the face of anxiety over change within and parallels between communities. It cannot, however, alter the increasing recognition of the comparative context of such appeals. The Theravada Buddhist who relies on the inerrant authority of the Pali canon, the fundamentalist Christian who bases his or her certainty on the verbally inspired Word of God, and the Wahhabi Muslim who cites the infallible Qur'an all may give each other pause—the more so as they become aware of extraordinarily impressive figures in their own traditions who have not shared their appeal to inerrantly authoritative, verbally inspired, and infallibly accurate texts. Similarly, appeals to supernatural events or precisely prescribed ritual practices or incommunicable self-authenticating experiences have less self-evident authority as there is increased awareness of differing interpretations within a single community and intriguing parallels in other traditions.

The effect of the historical and cross-cultural awareness is, then, frequently—even characteristically and in the end perhaps unavoidably—to call into question every appeal to a putatively inerrant authority. Awareness that has a comparative dimension and in that comparison is not only appreciative but also critical and self-critical in effect relativizes every such appeal. Diversity within a tradition renders problematical every sharply delineated standard of orthodoxy; and comparison among communities invites appeal to considerations not confined to any one tradition. Thus in practice even if not consistently in theory, the authority of any one tradition is subjected to appraisal on the basis of criteria that are arguably applicable over time and across traditions. The criteria on which such comparative appraisal is based are themselves subject to evaluation. There is not surprisingly also a plurality of positions on the issue of how most adequately to construe those criteria. But however diverse may be the specific criteria employed, they are all expressions of the general recognition that appeal to the authority of tradition alone does not suffice.

Here again, the novelty of the contemporary situation should not be overstated. Even cursory reading in the history of any religious community offers ample evidence that the truth of particular positions has been commended not only through appeals to traditional authorities but also through claims to illumine and in turn influence contemporary experience. References to the tradition and either implicit or explicit claims to represent that tradition on the one hand and arguments about the capacity to interpret and shape life today on the other of course appear in greatly differing ratios. But both forms of appeal are almost always present. In Christian traditions, for example, dogmatic and philosophical theology suggest poles between which there is a spectrum of approaches. Even in those traditions for which the designation "dogmatic" is invariably pejorative, there is also a combining of appeals to authoritative traditions and contemporary experience. Similarly, the most insistently dogmatic theology still at least tacitly claims to focus and clarify the ultimately crucial features of lived experience.

But while claims to illumine and influence contemporary experience have ample precedents in virtually all religious traditions, such claims have not been the focus of attention to the extent that they are in the context of increased awareness of change within and parallels between communities. As this double awareness in effect relativizes the authority of tradition, it at the same time increases the force of claims to interpret and in turn shape the whole of human experience. As a result, the question of criteria for adjudicating the relative adequacy of such claims becomes an inescapable issue for theology and its counterparts in nontheistic traditions.

The criteria employed must address the two sets of considerations implied in references not only to interpreting but also to shaping the whole of human experience. The criteria must, in short, focus attention on both descriptive and normative adequacy.

To aspire to interpret the whole of human experience entails a commitment to comprehensiveness that precludes retreat into a private or even a socially and culturally provincial sphere. Standards of descriptive adequacy thus seek to measure the extent and the depth to which the symbolic resources of a tradition have the capacity to incorporate into that frame of reference any and every datum of experience. Included here are, of course, the perennial questions, crises, and transitions that all religious traditions address: the relationship of the human to the natural, the cosmic, the ultimate; the realities of evil and suffering, of compassion and liberation; the meaning of life itself from birth through the struggles for and support of various communities to its end in individual and perhaps also collective death. But also included are particular historical developments—the missionary success of Islam, the economic power of capitalism, techniques for family planning and organ transplants, the possibility of nuclear annihilation. The criterion of adequacy to experience measures the capacity to interpret this entire range of data through the symbolic resources of the tradition, a capacity that in turn requires the vitality to accommodate new insights not anticipated in the tradition itself.

Important as is the capacity to interpret all of life, this descriptive adequacy is incomplete apart from its normative dimension. Indeed, mutual assessment of religious positions probably more often than not focuses on this dimension of implications for shaping the world. What is the hierarchy of values presupposed in religious positions that take the goal of religious discipline or devotion to be deliverance to a realm or an existence sharply distinguished from life in space and time? What are the consequences of construing the individual self as an illusion or as an infinitely valuable personality with an eternal destiny or as only provisionally discrete from the ultimate reality of which it is an expression? What is the impact on human being and value of trust in a deity who governs the whole of history or of commitment to a moral order that elicits fervent obedience or of insight into the ultimate emptiness of all reality?

COMMITMENT AND CHANGE IN
RELIGIOUS COMMUNITIES

Interaction among traditions that includes both comparative understanding and also at least tacit mutual appraisal will not, of course, reach easy or early agreement on judgments of relative descriptive and normative adequacy. Indeed, the least of the benefits of such interaction is any anticipated agreement. But what may and will occur is an acceleration of the ongoing process of development within each of the communities involved. For example, members of a community may discover that their tradition has attended insufficiently to the implications of contemporary astronomy or physics or genetics in its representation of the human condition and may, therefore, seek to take those data more thoroughly into account. Others may work to develop new emphases to counteract traditional tendencies toward tolerating or even legitimating social inequities which on reflection they do not want to affirm. Still others may conclude that the insistent iconoclasm of their traditions requires rethinking in view of the beauty of painting and sculpture evident in other communities but proscribed from theirs.

Such interaction and change do not require prior agreement on criteria for mutual appraisal. Instead, members of the various communities may bring to the process quite different and perhaps very particular criteria for assessing descriptive and normative adequacy. Differences in the criteria employed are not, however, disabling insofar as the initial and probably most crucial outcome of the process is change in one's own position. For in the case of such reflexive change, the criteria guiding the process are precisely the ones that are compelling to those who are modifying or developing their own positions.

Nor does this process of reflexive change—change in one's own position—preclude two other responses to interaction among traditions: a bracketing of the question of relative adequacy in favor of a scrupulous recording of positions in their historical particularity; and conversion from one community to the other. Those responses have been and may well continue to be frequent and influential. But neither a programmatic resistance to allowing judgments of adequacy nor an insistence on transferring allegiance from one tradition to another will eliminate the ongoing and almost certainly accelerating process of reflexive change already under way among all traditions as they participate together in an increasingly common history.

The process of interaction among communities may be especially influential insofar as it serves to intensify the self-consciousness of minority or even submerged tendencies in a tradition. Hence the result of such interaction may be an increase in the diversity within communities. For example, traditions that have focused almost exclusively on petitionary prayer may recover patterns of meditation and contemplation through contact with communities that have centered spiritual discipline on such practices. Or communities that have emphasized individual religious attainment may through interaction with other religious or secular traditions develop resources for supporting a sense of corporate responsibility. But each such provisional increase in diversity also affords the prospect of a commonality transcending traditional divisions as members of the various communities reinterpret and even modify their positions so as to accommodate further ranges of experience.

There are, of course, limits to the elasticity and adaptability of religious traditions. Thinkers may simply ignore those limits. They may, that is, commend the positions they advance exclusively on the basis of their capacity to interpret and their power to shape human experience as such, quite apart from any special reference to particular religious traditions. But for those theologians and their counterparts in nontheistic traditions who do claim to represent a particular religious community, the situation is more complex. On the one hand, they maintain that the position they hold satisfies the need for orientation and response in the contemporary world. On the other hand, they also affirm that position as consistent with and expressive of the traditions they claim to represent. In sum, they interpret and in turn shape contemporary experience through the symbolic resources of particular traditions, which they receive from others, to which they contribute, and for which they then take responsibility.

This ongoing process is what I called appropriation of traditions in chapter 1. It is the process through which participants in religious communities identify with and live out of the traditions of those communities: they make those traditions their own. In the context of increased awareness of change within and parallels between religious communities, this process is more and more self-consciously both comparative and critical. It is therefore not simply acceptance of what is passed on through authoritative channels. Instead, appropriation is a constructive process requiring critical engagement with the commitments of a particular community and comparative assessment of alternative positions in multiple traditions. As such, this process is both a crucial dimension of the comparative history of religions and a critically important resource for religious communities worldwide.

PART TWO

Commitment and Social Practice

5

The Changing Role of
Religion in Society

In addressing the question of commitment in the context of cultural pluralism and historical relativism, the foregoing chapters illustrate again and again that this question unavoidably involves interconnections between religious life and thought and other domains of personal, social, and cultural experience. The extended consideration in chapters 1 and 2 of issues raised by feminism and by limits to growth exemplify such interconnections. So, too, do the prospects for collaboration among religious communities—prospects noted explicitly at the close of chapter 3 and presupposed in the entire line of argument in chapter 4.

This interrelatedness of commitment and public issues is certainly not a new development. In even the most spiritually focused sectarian communities, religious commitment has always carried implications for other domains of life; and whether or not the reciprocal influence has been acknowledged, broader social ideas and institutions have also had their impact on such communities. But despite the constant of mutual influence, the dominant pattern of relationship between religious commitment and public issues has changed over time and in particular has undergone a decisive shift in the course of the past several centuries.

History does not deal kindly with those who are convinced that their situation is decisively new and different. The reason is a good one: there are so many such people, and they are almost always wrong. But despite my acute awareness of being in bad company,

I am persuaded that the role of religion today is not merely incidentally but rather systematically different from the dominant pattern of the major world religions—a pattern that fundamentally
shaped human religious experience for some two thousand years,
up to and including the recent past. I realize that all such large
claims are suspect. Accordingly, I will proceed systematically and
in measured steps even though this approach will entail some
repetition of points also registered in preceding chapters. First, I
will outline what I am calling the dominant pattern of the major
world religions. Then I will show how this pattern contrasts with
the orientation not only of traditions that antedate what have become the major world religions but also of much recent religious
life and thought. Finally, I will argue that while straightforward
acknowledgment of this fundamental shift from the dominant orientation of the major world religions is threatening, it also offers
the promise of opportunities that religious communities should
embrace.

ORIENTATION TO SALVATION
BEYOND THIS WORLD

What I am calling the dominant pattern of the major world religions
is an orientation to salvation beyond this world. In the history of
most of Christian piety and theology, the goal of the religious life
has been salvation quite explicitly distinguished from historical
existence: heaven over against earth or the beatific vision of God
in contrast to the blindness of the world. To focus on deliverance
from historical existence as the goal of faith or devotion or discipline
is also a pervasive orientation in major forms of Hindu, Buddhist,
Muslim, and other religious traditions. The representations of this
goal vary enormously, as does reflection on the relationship between the otherness toward which faith or devotion or discipline
is oriented and ordinary life in space and time. But the persistence
of the pattern is nonetheless—or all the more—striking.[1]

Examples like those noted in previous chapters illustrate the
point. Not surprisingly, in view of their shared history, the pattern
of polarity in Christian traditions is also evident and even accentuated in Islam: Allah utterly transcends the world; this life is
emphatically affirmed and yet is still radically inferior to the eternal

destiny for which it prepares. In the case of Hindu traditions, there is staggering variety. Yet in and through that diversity, virtual unanimity emerges in representing the goal of the religious life as the attainment of *moksha*—that is, deliverance from *samsara*, the round of birth and death that constitutes ordinary historical life. In Buddhist history, the situation is even more complex because of the range of geography and culture involved. But in this case as well, orientation toward deliverance from ordinary historical existence is a persistent pattern. An example deeply rooted in Indian society and therefore recurrent throughout Buddhist literature is the metaphor of the raft that bears the disciple or devotee to the other shore, to *nirvana* over against *samsara*. So fundamental is this metaphor that it has become a way of naming the most basic division among Buddhist traditions: the Mahayana (literally, the large raft) call their opponents the Hinayana (the small or narrow raft)—a designation that those opponents, who call their tradition Theravada (the way of the elders), understandably prefer not to use. To note a further example, this time one prevalent in East Asia, for the numerous schools of Pure Land Buddhism, the goal of life is represented as rebirth in the Western paradise of Amida, a realm purified of the defilements of ordinary historical existence.

Paradoxically, this orientation across religious traditions to salvation beyond this world has resulted in great temporal power. It has invited—and has almost always been correlative with—appeals to absolute or ultimate truth revealed from that other realm. The result is the authority that comes from the claim to insight or revelation that transcends ordinary modes of experience or knowledge. The authority of the Bible, the Qur'an, and the Pali Canon illustrate the force of this claim.

This contrast between ordinary and extraordinary knowledge or experience has its counterpart in social roles. Renunciation of possessions and sexual relationships in favor of withdrawal from the world pose the sharpest contrast to ordinary social expectations. It is accordingly not surprising that hermits, ascetic wanderers, and monastic communities appear in traditions that focus on salvation beyond this world. Such traditions also allow for what are agreed to be lesser forms of commitment, which people with occupational and family responsibilities may meet. But the standard against which this more limited commitment is measured is characteristically that of the hermit, ascetic, or monk who focuses all available

energy on attaining release from entanglement in historical existence and salvation in that other realm.

The institutional expressions of orientation to salvation beyond
this world are quite varied. The starkest instance is the network of
support that even a forest hermit or desert ascetic requires for his
(and very occasionally her) disciplined pursuit of final truth and
liberation. Still sharply set off from ordinary life but less austere
are monastic communities as they developed especially in Buddhism and Christianity. Also set over against established patterns
but in this case fundamentally concerned about changing them are
religious roles like that of biblical prophecy and other religiously
influenced movements for reform that appeal to transcendent standards—the divine word or the mandate of heaven, for example—
to support specific criticism of established structures or policies,
political leaders, or even religious figures who have become too
completely entangled in worldly affairs. Finally, very much closer
to the established patterns of ordinary historical life but still in
principle distinguished from the secular order are religious bodies
that include both celibate priests and lay members who have occupational and family responsibilities but who also have a religious
identity beyond those worldly obligations.

Each of the major world religions offers instances of these institutional expressions of orientation to salvation beyond this world.
But in view of its position as the background or even the foundation
for the development of the modern West, medieval Christianity
may serve as a summary illustration. In any case, medieval Christianity impressively exemplifies the ways in which orientation to
salvation beyond this world shaped the identities not only of religious movements and institutions but also of society as a whole.
Each member of the church after baptism was a new person, the
true self destined for eternal bliss. This religious identity was in
principle distinguished from social roles in the secular order. Similarly, the medieval church was the authoritative institutional base
that served as the mediator to transcendent reality. The church was
not, of course, simply opposed to the secular order. Indeed, it
provided a comprehensive rationale for the central values of medieval culture and thereby legitimated existing social patterns very
effectively. But the social patterns that the church reinforced included an explicitly articulated authority for religious as distinguished from secular power. The pope personified this authority

over against the emperor: the ultimate power of the church as keeper of the keys of the eternal or heavenly kingdom in contrast to the merely temporal aims of every earthly power.

OTHER PATTERNS OF ORIENTATION

Precisely because orientation toward salvation beyond this world has been so pronounced a feature of the major world religions, it has tended to overshadow or obscure other patterns. For example, the available evidence indicates that before the first millenium B.C.E. there was little denigration of this world in favor of deliverance to some other realm, even when there was affirmation of existence after death. Instead, myths were related to specific objects or events and rituals enacted those myths for the benefit of this life, albeit this life construed as encompassing the ancestors and spirits and gods and all other existing entities.[2] In the further history of religious traditions, this pattern has, however, often been assimilated to or even submerged into orientation toward salvation in another realm.

Similarly, over the course of the last three centuries and especially in the last century and a half, the world view informing interpretations of Christianity as oriented to salvation beyond this world has become increasingly dubious to increasing numbers of people. Initially, a small stratum of intellectuals criticized religious beliefs as incompatible with modernity. With the spread of education and the rise in social expectations from the seventeenth century onward, a larger and larger proportion of the population has, however, come to share this disenchantment with traditional interpretations of Christian symbolism and has found orientation toward another realm or the next life to be neither plausible nor satisfying.

The shift away from orientation toward another realm has frequently been presumed to be a rejection of religion as such. This presumption is not surprising in view of the prevalence of orientation to salvation beyond this world both in Christian history and still in much contemporary piety. But the result nonetheless is that even when there are few if any indications of orientation toward salvation beyond this world, religious views are often construed as including this reference. In the case of believers, affirmation of traditional formulations and assent to apparently accepted interpretations may govern verbal expressions even when belief in salvation beyond this world has no discernible impact on their style of life or behavior. At the same time, interpretations of religious symbolism that do not focus on salvation beyond this world may be repudiated as revisionist or dismissed as only accommodating to the pressures of the prevailing culture.

This tendency to suppress alternative patterns of interpretation or to define them as deficient versions of religion underestimates the diversity and the capacity for change in religious traditions. It also obscures significant common ground among otherwise quite disparate positions. Especially noteworthy in this respect is the at least partial parallel between influential views in the post–Enlightenment West and the basic orientation of societies prior to the emergence and outside the area of impact of the major world religions. This parallel is significant because it offers widespread illustrations of religious positions that do not focus on the goal of deliverance from historical existence. The parallel—including the extent to which it is only partial—is, furthermore, directly relevant to understanding the role of religion in contemporary society.

THE ROLE OF RELIGION TODAY

Both the similarities and the differences between the modern West and societies for which salvation beyond this world has never been a central concern are illuminating for understanding the role of religion today. The similarities may be formulated as a contrast to the pattern of medieval Christendom. Neither in the modern West nor in societies for which salvation beyond this world has never been a central concern is religion identified with a single clearly differentiated institution, as it is in medieval Christendom. Instead, in both cases, religious impulses, images, and ideas tend to be diffused throughout the social system.

But societies that have no prior tradition of central concern for salvation beyond this world also offer a striking point of contrast on the question of the role of religion in relation to the social order. When there is no prior tradition of salvation beyond this world, there also typically is no clear differentiation between the religious and other social sectors. To put the point with reference to its least elaborated instance, in many Australian and African tribal societies, the priest and the king are the same person. Accordingly, religion does not have a discrete institutional base but instead is a dimension of other variables in the social order.

In this situation, the central and perhaps exclusive role of religion is to express a sense of common identity and to reinforce the patterns that provide cohesion for the social unit as a whole. Religion has no point of leverage over against the pattern of social arrangements and personal roles because it is completely absorbed into or is exclusively a dimension of those arrangements. Myths interpret the origins and the meaning of the patterns that govern the society as it is; and rituals reenact those myths in the sacred ceremonies of the society. But there is no systematic grounding for appeals to standards understood as transcending those patterns and providing a basis for assessing them critically.

As I attempted to indicate in my summary outline of their orientation toward salvation beyond this world, the dominant forms of the major world religions provide a significant contrast at precisely this point. The other realm to which such symbol systems direct attention stands over against all of historical existence. In comparison to that realm, all extant social arrangements are deemed deficient and all socially ascribed roles are at most provisionally affirmed. Religion certainly continues to contribute to integrating society and to articulating and sustaining cultural values. But there are also standards in principle not subject to the control of political and other nonreligious authorities.

That this entire tradition of both interpretation and institutional patterns is presupposed in the further development of the role of religion in society sets the contemporary situation apart from all positions that do not stand on the foundation of a prior orientation toward salvation beyond this world. As a result of this prior tradition, contemporary religious symbolism offers the capacity to stand over against and critically evaluate established personal, social, and cultural patterns. The world view informing interpretations of religious symbolism that focus on salvation in another realm may no longer be compelling for increasing numbers of people. But the symbolism itself continues to provide resources for envisioning alternatives and therefore need not have the effect of simply interpreting and reinforcing society as it is. Indeed, precisely this symbolism in the diverse forms in which it is expressed in the various religious traditions is an often all but forgotten underlying source of even many militantly secular traditions of social criticism.

To call attention to this capacity to envision alternatives and stand over against established patterns is not to reduce the role of religion to that of social criticism. Religious symbol systems continue to provide a comprehensive frame of reference for individuals and communities. Such symbol systems are central to the process of interpreting and in turn shaping the experience of all who struggle to affirm a religious identity distinguished from the roles offered or imposed by the prevailing secular culture. In the shared life of religious communities, mythic patterns continue to be enacted in rituals that embody the truth passed on in the particular traditions of those communities. In the case of Christian churches, for example, the sacraments of the eucharist or communion and baptism continue to be the central forms of this life. So, too, religious instruction in general and preaching in particular contribute to the ongoing nourishment of religious values and commitments. Perhaps most crucially of all, the common life of a particular religious community provides a context for mutual support and shared concern that is desperately needed in an atomistically individualistic consumer society and mass culture.

All of these contributions of religion to human life are of fundamental importance and therefore also of continuing significance for religious communities. They in effect testify to the ongoing power of deeply rooted patterns across religious traditions. They do not, however, identify what is distinctive about the role of religion in contemporary society.

What does distinguish this relatively recent role for religion may be summarized through a recapitulation of its similarities with and differences from the patterns of the past. Like relatively undifferentiated societies that do not denigrate this world in favor of salvation in another realm, religion in contemporary society, in practice even if not always in theory, attends centrally to life in this world. In contrast to the dominant pattern of the major world religions, this orientation involves a shift from a focus on salvation beyond this world to a central concern for natural and historical life on earth. It also tends toward a diffusion of religion throughout the society rather than its identification with a single clearly differentiated institution. But unlike its role in relatively undifferentiated societies, religion today includes resources for criticism based on the tension entailed in appeals to standards that transcend historical attainments and against which established structures and socially ascribed roles are deemed deficient. What is distinctive about the role of religion in contemporary society is, in short, that it is both this-worldly and critical.

RELIGIOUS COMMITMENT AS THIS-WORLDLY AND CRITICAL

This shift in orientation from a focus on salvation beyond this world to a central and critical concern for life on earth is evident across traditions. Illustrations from Christian thought and practice include the increasingly open political involvement of both Protestant Evangelicals and Roman Catholic bishops in recent years in this country and the even greater activism of, for example, Presbyterians in Korea and Catholics in Central America and the Philippines. Similarly engaged in social movements are Theravada Buddhists in Sri Lanka and Thailand or some of the new forms of Buddhism—the Risho Kosei-Kai, for example—in Japan. Also widespread is Muslim involvement in social and political action, as crosscurrents in Iran, Afghanistan, and Malaysia illustrate in quite different ways. In many if not most such movements, appeals to transcendent truth and even to destined salvation beyond this world continue to figure in the rhetoric employed. But the effect nonetheless is to focus on critical engagement with this-worldly issues.

The refocusing of religious vision from salvation beyond this world to concern for natural and historical life that distinguishes the role of religion today from the dominant orientation of the major world religions poses very fundamental challenges for religious communities. As I have noted, orientation toward salvation beyond this world invites appeal to authoritative truth revealed from that other realm and supports a central institutional locus to serve as representative of and mediator to that other realm. Conversely, erosion of that double base of authority and social standing constitutes a threat to the very viability of religious communities.

At the same time, straightforward acknowledgment of this refocusing of religious vision offers substantial opportunities for religious communities to move away from some debilitating patterns of the past. For centuries, energy has been directed toward suppressing awareness of this fundamental shift in religious orientation. The results have been perverse. Individuals have in effect

compartmentalized their religious beliefs as private matters separate from increasing ranges of experience to which those beliefs
seemed to have little connection. Religious communities have become marginalized in institutional terms and, at least in part because of conflicts over the priority of salvation beyond this world,
have been insecure in developing alternative approaches to shaping
natural and historical life. Secular institutions, increasingly cut off
from the religious roots that nourished their underlying values,
have been preoccupied more and more exclusively with technical
and bureaucratic solutions to social problems.

To confront and seek to reverse such debilitating patterns requires
an intentional reconnecting of religious thought to those disciplines
from which it has become dismembered in the ongoing differentiation of Western intellectual life. Put negatively, this reconnecting
means resisting defensive strategies designed to buttress an allegedly unassailable position—typically one founded on revelation
from beyond this world—over against other methods of investi-
gation. Put positively, it entails relating the symbolic resources of
religious traditions to the entire range of disciplines not only in the
humanities but also in the social and natural sciences. Only this
approach can overcome the impoverishment of a theology that
resorts to only the most abstract or general formulations in order
to avoid intruding onto the terrain of other domains of inquiry.
This approach can overcome such impoverishment because it re-
claims a stake in the concrete and particular data of natural and
historical life that have been ceded to other disciplines. All those
data—rather than only what is affirmed as beyond the empirical—
must again in principle be included in the purview of religion. Only
then may religious thought contribute to the ongoing development
of the particular symbol systems through which human communities interpret and in turn shape all of experience.

As with religious thought, so with religious practice, what is
needed is an overcoming of a tendency to set religious discipline
over against historical life. The most insightful and influential contemporary writers on spirituality are at least tacitly aware of the
need to relate spiritual discipline to concern for this world. Indeed,
even when advocates of very traditional spirituality insist that its
central goal is preparation for salvation beyond this world, they
still attend to its implications for life here and now and not infrequently commend it on that basis. In any case, what is required is

rigorous thought and disciplined practice in developing a spirituality that integrates religious commitment with vigorous concern for corporate historical life and does so without the apologies that result when salvation beyond this world is taken to be the only finally legitimate goal of such commitment.

Religious thought and practice recast in this direction unavoidably entail attention to the social implications of religious commitment. Among those implications is the requirement that commitment be resolutely critical of established structures because they are unavoidably deficient when measured against standards that transcend historical attainments. But also required in this recast religious thought and practice is the attempt to express shared values for communities that aspire to be inclusive—an attempt desperately needed in our society today.

Such attention to social issues is certainly not confined to any one religious tradition. Indeed, as I noted in chapter 3, collaboration among religious communities in addressing urgent global threats like nuclear war or world hunger is an intriguing indication of the degree to which the major world religions share in the shift to a critical and this-worldly orientation. The struggle to articulate and support common positions on such issues in effect participates in expressing shared values around which inclusive communities may form. This movement toward collaboration across traditional divisions is, therefore, salutary not only in its own right but also because it embodies the critical and this-worldly tendencies that offer the most promising prospect for revitalizing the role of religion in contemporary society.

6

Communities of Faith/ Communities of Learning

The opportunity—and the need—for collaboration across established divisions is not confined to relations among the various religious communities. There is a parallel need and opportunity in the relations of religious to educational institutions. In view of the long history of mutual dependence between religion and education, it may seem paradoxical to refer to the need and the opportunity for collaboration. But despite—and in part perhaps because of— this long history of interaction and mutual support or even sponsorship, there is strong resistance to such collaboration. Accordingly, I will begin with an examination of the mutual perceptions of communities of faith and communities of learning that inhibit and often block a sense of shared purpose. I will then indicate an approach that brings into view the common ground on which communities of faith and communities of learning stand. Finally, I will indicate how this common ground provides a vantage point or a staging area from which communities of faith and communities of learning can and should engage pressing moral issues facing all of us.

BLIND CONVICTION VS. DISPASSIONATE
INQUIRY

The question of the relationship between communities of faith and communities of learning typically generates more heat than light because it is too often framed with reference to two caricatures. The caricatures result from the mutual stereotyping in which communities of faith and communities of learning indulge.

One caricature is that of communities of faith as unavoidably appealing to unquestioned dogma or some other infallible authority. To use all the stereotypes, communities of faith are portrayed as not only appealing to authorities they allege to be infallible but also as in effect engaging in uncritical propaganda aimed at engendering blind conviction. Communities of faith may still be held to serve a useful purpose in shaping a corporate identity and shared values for their members. To borrow a category from the sociology of knowledge, communities of faith may provide a plausibility structure on the basis of which their members interpret and act in their world. But useful as serving such purposes may be, the starting point, the procedures, and the warrants for this enterprise are construed as fundamentally different from the quest for knowledge that characterizes communities of learning.

The other caricature is the mirror image of this one. It is, however, more often than not a self-caricature rather than a stereotype imposed by others. Precisely to assert its autonomy over against allegedly infallible authorities and uncritical propaganda and blind allegiance, this position characterizes itself, or at least allows itself to be characterized, as objective and dispassionate and even value-free inquiry. The heir and guardian of scientific method, the community of learning in this view stands proudly on the record of the achievements of the Western university. Not only the accomplishments of the natural sciences and their technological application but also the enormous accumulation of philological and historical data and the increasingly sophisticated understanding of personal, social, and cultural processes testify to the vitality of this tradition of inquiry. Even the scientific study of religion finds its place here, as long as the investigator does not allow any values or commitments of his or her own to intrude on the process of examination or distort the objectivity of the findings.

Like all caricatures, these two representations of communities of faith and communities of learning contain more than a grain of truth. Certainly there are significant differences in the purposes and procedures of the two communities. But there are equally certainly very substantial similarities which stereotyped characterizations serve only to obscure.

The inadequacies of the two caricatures as descriptions of communities of faith and communities of learning are perhaps most visible when we look at the theory of knowledge that both of them imply. At this point the assumptions underlying the two quite different stereotypes are, ironically, very similar. Consequently, the deficiencies in their common assumptions about the nature and limits of knowledge may serve to epitomize the inadequacies in both characterizations. Indeed, their shared but in the end untenable premises about the nature and limits of knowledge in part account for the intractability of most debates between the two positions, whether those debates be framed as between the church and the university, faith and reason, or religion and science.

RELATIVISM AND DOGMATISM

The most comprehensive and historically the most influential statement of the theory of knowledge that informs both positions is Immanuel Kant's *Critique of Pure Reason*. Kant was enormously impressed with the achievement of Newtonian physics in establishing a secure foundation for knowledge that was both replicable and cumulative. At the same time, he was very concerned to safeguard the claims of what he called rational faith and morality. He therefore set himself the double objective of specifying the conditions of the possibility of the knowledge of the natural sciences while simultaneously identifying the limits of such knowledge—limits that would, as he wrote in the preface to the second edition of the *Critique of Pure Reason*, "make room for *faith*."[1]

Kant specified the conditions of knowledge so that it was limited to empirical phenomena. Within this spatial and temporal frame of reference, there is knowledge that Kant defended as objective in the sense that it is universal and necessary for all human subjects. But precisely because this knowledge presupposes the human perceptual and conceptual constitution, it is limited to empirical data. In Kant's terms, it cannot attain to the noumenal as opposed to the phenomenal realm, or to the thing in itself as opposed to appearances in space and time. About any such further realm or reality, the human subject can claim no knowledge whatsoever. That is instead the arena for faith.

The model of knowing is, then, one of inviolable limits, of insurmountable barriers, which confine human knowers to the world of appearances and separate them programmatically from the real as such. It is as if we human knowers are confined in a sealed room. We can know everything inside of that room in minute detail. But the walls are impenetrable. We have a clear sense that they are there. We can and do bang into them, and we infer or assume that they divide us from a further realm that in effect surrounds us on all sides. But we have no access whatsoever to that other realm.

This model is not, of course, confined to Kant. Since 1781, when the *Critique of Pure Reason* was published, Kant's analysis has had enormous influence. But less precisely and systematically formulated variants on this general pattern had also characterized much of Western reflection on the nature and limits of knowledge in earlier periods. A similar tendency is evident in other cultures as well. In Oriental philosophy, for example, the distinction between a world of appearances and the ultimate reality beyond those appearances dominates Hindu traditions and is also very much in evidence in Buddhist reflection.

Despite innumerable other instances, Kant's line of reasoning is nonetheless a convenient point of reference because it is so often at least tacitly assumed in continuing Western formulations of a defense either of faith against the corrosive influence of learning or of learning against the pretensions of faith. In the former case—that is, in defenses of faith—the formulation may not unfairly be characterized as dogmatic. In the latter case—that is, in defenses of learning—the position is relativistic. But both positions explicitly or implicitly share a theory of knowledge with strong family resemblances to that of Kant.

The connection is more straightforward in the case of relativism. Kant's contention that we can never, so to speak, get behind the phenomenal realm or the world of appearances to the noumenal realm or things as they are in themselves means that we have no access whatsoever from empirical knowledge to reality as such. As a result, we have no basis in our empirical knowledge for preferring any one claim to know about reality over other such claims. Instead, all knowledge is by definition empirical and therefore in principle absolutely incommensurable with the real as such. Because there is no possible way of adjudicating the relative merits of such competing positions, the only theoretically defensible position appears to be an unqualified relativism.

Paradoxically, this line of reasoning, which may eventuate in a defense of unqualified relativism, may also be enlisted in support of positions that, from this base, claim to be immune to the corrosive effect of precisely such relativism. The most influential twentieth-century Christian illustration of this claim is the line of argument Karl Barth advanced in his *The Epistle to the Romans,* first published in 1918. Barth includes Christianity with all other religious traditions as historically relative expressions of human arrogance forever doomed to failure in their attempts to attain to the truth of God. But Barth then introduces a distinction between revealed Christian faith or the Gospel on the one hand and Christianity as one more historically relative human religious tradition on the other. He asserts that Christian faith or the Gospel is not a human creation but is rather the direct expression of the action of God. As such, it must be systematically distinguished from all historically relative human traditions, including Christianity. As a result, divine revelation alone is said to provide access to that truth of God from which every human effort to know is infinitely distant.[2]

Kant himself would no doubt be chagrined to see his reflection on the limits of theoretical reason employed in the service of either unqualified relativism or dogmatic theology. After all, his efforts were directed toward establishing the objectivity of empirical knowledge and protecting the claims of rational or moral religion. But he has innumerable heirs who do not share his confidence about grounding religion in moral practice but who do find compelling his criticism of claims to know the real as such. While they agree with his demolition of the structures of metaphysics and theology, they then conclude that they cannot live in the home he himself constructed on the old foundation. The result is the leveled foundation of complete relativism—except for those extraordinarily enterprising souls who erect a new dogmatic edifice in the place of the old ruins.

Not surprisingly, caricatures often result when the representations that communities of faith and communities of learning have of each other presuppose such formulations of dogmatic theology and unqualified relativism. The fact that serious thinkers have espoused both positions does not alter this situation. Indeed, the fact that both positions are in significant respects important and true does not alter the temptation to caricature and mutual stereotyping. The reason is that no matter how true they are, both positions also lend themselves very readily to appearing arbitrary and contrived. To contend that the relativity of all perspectives precludes discrimination among positions because they are all absolutely incommensurable with the real seems somehow arbitrary. Similarly, to distinguish the revelation of God proclaimed in the Christian Gospel from all religion seems contrived. And in both cases, the sense of artificiality is justified because the broadly Kantian theory of knowledge informing those positions is untenable.

CRITICAL RELATIVISM

Kant's theory of knowledge has continued to be enormously influential for the past two centuries. But that enormous influence notwithstanding, the central difficulty of this theory of knowledge was identified even before Kant's death. It was specified most cogently in the definitive and in my view incontrovertible critique of Kant's position developed by G. W. F. Hegel.

Hegel again and again argued that the dichotomy between phenomenal knowledge and noumenal reality is untenable in the strict sense that it cannot be formulated without contradiction. Insofar as human subjects conceive of and talk about the thing in itself or noumenal reality, they already relate it to other forms of awareness or consciousness including that of empirical objects. There is, in short, no absolute distinction between what is available to human knowing and reality as such. Instead, all claims to knowledge are more or less successful attempts to grasp or comprehend the real itself. It is, to be sure, useful and even necessary to distinguish between the object as it is in the consciousness of the knower and the thing in itself. But while the intention of this distinction is to call attention to the limitations of a given claim to knowledge, its effect is to drive the knower toward more adequate comprehension. The result is an ongoing process of interaction between the knower and the real, a process that in principle acknowledges no limits even if in practice it can never attain that ideal of totally adequate comprehension, which Hegel termed "absolute knowledge" or "the truth."[3]

The model of knowing implicit in this view is, then, quite different from that of a constant coming up against the fixed walls of a sealed room. Instead, a more appropriate picture is a spider at work weaving its web. The spider spins to extend its reach, thread by thread, as it seeks to grasp whatever enters its domain. So, too, we human knowers reach out to sense and to understand what is around us. In German, the metaphor of grasping (as when we take hold of an object in our hands) is preserved in the word for thinking and thought: *"begreifen"* and *"Begriff."* In English, the metaphor is less evident because it depends on the Latin, but "conceive" and "conception" similarly derive from the root that means to take up or to grasp. In sum, when we know, we are not merely perceiving the world of appearances but are struggling to grasp the real as such.

This Hegelian critique of Kant provides resources for moving beyond the deficient premises of both theological dogmatism and unqualified relativism to a third, more adequate position. This third position acknowledges the truth of relativism. It recognizes the rootedness of every position in particular personal, social, and cultural conditions. It also agrees with dogmatic theology in insisting that judgments as to truth and validity are not only possible but necessary. The result of this double awareness is to invite and even require a comparative and critical stance toward all claims, including one's own. Insofar as various partial and incomplete perspectives are attempts at grasping or comprehending the one reality there is, judgments as to their relative measure of validity become unavoidable. The task of articulating and defending criteria for this critical and comparative enterprise is, to be sure, extremely complex and itself subject to appraisal. But because the reality toward which claims of truth are directed is not by definition inaccessible, this task is not proscribed in principle.

This third position bears directly on the question of the relationship of communities of faith to communities of learning because it describes the process in which both kinds of communities participate. But in the past, the extent of this common ground has been obscured. Communities of faith, aware of their own particular commitments, have simply affirmed just that particularity as universally true and therefore destined to displace the particular traditions of others. In contrast, communities of learning have tended to be unaware of their own particularity and consequently presumed somewhat complacently that their point of view provided a universally valid frame of reference for understanding the provincial perspectives of all others. In both cases, therefore, the effect has been to work against an approach that is inclusively comparative and critical in the sense that one's own perspective is among the traditions scrutinized.

What is needed is an understanding of communities of faith and communities of learning that is in this sense inclusively comparative and critical. Such an understanding entails self-criticism as a central feature of the process of interaction among traditions. This self-criticism is not an end in itself but rather a means to increasingly adequate awareness of both self and other—a sharper sense of particular identity, together with a more comprehensive knowledge of the orientations of others. Because this comparative and critical understanding includes a reflexive dimension, it is an active process of engagement that intimately involves our own values and commitments. We are in effect participating in what I, in previous chapters, have termed the critical appropriation of traditions, traditions that we in one way or another make our own as we seek to understand them.

As I have attempted to illustrate with a variety of examples, this process of appropriation demands of us the struggle not only to understand but also to evaluate, perhaps to criticize, and then in some sense to act upon the traditions in which we participate. We cannot avoid this demand because all of us orient ourselves with reference to the resources of one tradition or another—or, more accurately, of multiple traditions as they interact. As we participate in various communities, we appropriate the symbolic resources of their traditions: stories, images, ideas, institutional patterns, norms, and injunctions. Through that process we interpret our experience and in turn allow it to be shaped in new directions.

Both communities of faith and communities of learning have distorted this process of appropriating traditions because they have tended to focus on the traditions involved more than on the process of appropriation. In the case of communities of faith, the result is a tendency to view the process simply as acceptance of what is passed on through what are taken to be authoritative channels. In the case of communities of learning, a more dynamic conception of changing traditions may be operative. But the traditions studied all too often are relegated either to the past or to another community. Over against both of these characteristically traditionalist orientations, appropriation can and should be construed as an active process in which traditions do not have automatic or unquestioned authority but nonetheless are accorded respect for their power to interpret and shape our ongoing experience.

BEYOND PROVINCIALISM AND PASSIVITY

As communities of faith and communities of learning together encounter the pressing issues confronting all of us on a global scale, we can no longer afford either the passivity or the provincialism that too often characterize both uncritical believers and self-satisfied intellectuals. Instead, we must appropriate the best of the traditions that have formed us so that we are enabled in turn to engage the challenges facing us with vision and energy, with wisdom and courage. To illustrate this process, I will sketch what I see as the most fundamental, the most deeply rooted, issue demanding our attention and include in the sketch an outline of the broad range of ramifications entailed in it.

The most fundamental challenge we face is to criticize and counter the pervasive and corrosive individualism of our prevailing culture. This individualism provides cultural legitimation for even the most extreme self-centered and narcissistic behavior. It in effect rationalizes indifference to the plight of others and exclusive preoccupation with one's own satisfaction because it takes the atomistic individual to be both primary and ultimate.

This individualism has a long and distinguished ancestry. Its deepest source lies in the religious conviction that the human self is of inestimable worth—is, indeed, the very image of the divine. In the West since the Enlightenment, this sense of the dignity of the individual has been expressed in and through an impressive range of secular developments. Instances include market capitalism as an economic order, contractual relations as the basis of the legal system, democratic government as a political pattern, and voluntary associations as a form of social organization. There is much of value in this interconnected set of developments. But even as we affirm the emergence of this self-conscious individualism, we cannot escape its increasingly corrosive effects on our corporate life.

Communities of faith have a special contribution to offer in criticizing this individualism because of the role that religious insights have played and continue to play in generating and sustaining an orientation that focuses on the value of the individual self. In contrast to the tendency to focus on individual fulfillment, whether in this life or the next, communities of faith must oppose any and every view that begins uncritically with separate selves and then almost unavoidably becomes preoccupied with achieving satisfaction for the self, including satisfying relationships as simply a means to this end. Over against this orientation, communities of faith must remind us all that we do not begin as separate entities, which then somehow must become connected. Instead, we are all members of a common body—a body that is broken, even fragmented, but that is also an expression of the finally all-inclusive divine-human community in which we live and move and have our being.

This vision of a finally all-inclusive community is only an attractive abstraction unless it is actualized in concrete historical institutions. Accordingly, particular communities of faith are indispensable as embodiments of the more inclusive reality in which they participate. To use Christian symbolism, we are incorporated into this body at baptism; and we celebrate both its brokenness and its wholeness whenever we participate in communion or the eucharist. Thus the central Christian affirmations and injunctions expressed in the sacraments of baptism and the eucharist stand firmly against the uncritical individualism of so much of our culture. They testify that this uncritical individualism—whether articulated in Protestant fundamentalism or secular humanism—is not only destructive in its consequences but also false in its premises. And that is a testimony our culture needs desperately to hear as it enshrines self-gratification on the altar of individualism.

Crucial as is this testimony of communities of faith, it must receive support as well from communities of learning. Communities of faith are called not only to live as members of a common body in a particular institution but also to participate in realizing the finally all-inclusive divine-human community envisioned as our destiny. The struggle to realize this inclusive community entails the need to engage complex intellectual issues and institutional relationships. Accordingly, it requires not only the vision and energy of communities of faith but also wisdom and courage from communities of learning.

The complexities involved in even conceiving—not to mention organizing—an all-inclusive community are evident in the simple fact that the most encompassing contemporary institutions tend to foster isolation rather than community. We are all too often isolated from one another even as more and more of us are related to each other through the imposing and even invading institutions that shape us all: big business, pervasive government, organized labor, and, perhaps most of all, the omnipresent media. Because we are so often related to each other through such bureaucratic institutions, we are constantly tempted to see each other and even ourselves as interchangeable entities. We are confronted with an enormous range of choices. Yet somehow, as we face more or less the same selection, we seem standardized more than individualized in our choosing. Institutional patterns developed to provide individual fulfillment paradoxically result in life-styles that are at one and the same time highly personalized and pretty much predictable.

The complexities only become more staggering when the situation is viewed globally. We may have intellectual, aesthetic, and even ethical aversions to the various secular adaptations of individualistic conceptions of salvation that are paraded through our consumer society and mass culture as we are invited to fulfill ourselves and are seduced into an endless preoccupation with satisfying desires masquerading as needs. But aversion must become opposition when focused on the indefensibly inequitable distribution of natural resources and human products. In this global context, commitment to inclusive human community requires programs for rectifying the inequities in existing patterns of resource allocation and use. To design and implement such programs is a formidable task. Indeed, in view of the forces arrayed against them, serious proposals for redistribution are in effect wagers against enormous odds.

Yet precisely because of this almost overwhelming array of complexities, we who are also in communities of learning must address the issues involved through the ways in which we conduct ourselves at the core of our common enterprise, namely, in our teaching and research. Here we need to respond to the double threat individualism poses for our emerging world culture. On the one hand, we must examine the social and cultural ramifications of modern Western individualism, with special attention to the issue of just distribution. On the other hand, we must call attention to the deeply problematic tendency to view human persons as interchangeable entities—a tendency that preoccupation with individual fulfillment fosters in our consumer society and mass culture.

Teaching and research across the curriculum can and should address this double threat. Study in the arts and humanities must intentionally and self-critically explore the images and ideals that have shaped and continue to shape our common life. But the social and natural sciences must also attend carefully and systematically to the ethical implications of their investigations. For example, future doctors should not complete their education without confronting such issues as equity in access to health care, trade-offs between extraordinary efforts to extend individual lives and systemic approaches in public health or preventive medicine, and the political influence of medical technology and health insurance interests. To take another example, our colleges and universities should require basic literacy in computer science of all graduates; but that basic literacy should include consideration of such issues as the preservation of privacy and the control of centralized information systems. Similarly, the grounding in economics necessary for intelligent participation in public life should include examination of such issues as the role of advertising in molding tastes and generating consumer demand, social costs of unplanned development and pollution, and the implication for Third World countries of some of the accounting practices of transnational corporations.

Addressing questions of this sort should not be confined to special courses devoted to ethics or comparative social values. There should certainly be such specialized courses. But questions of value should also be addressed explicitly and systematically throughout the curriculum. Only then do we in communities of learning contribute centrally to meeting the moral challenges confronting all of us on a global scale. And only then do we participate effectively in the comparative and critical appropriation of the traditions that we inherit and in turn hand on. Because communities of learning share in this process of comparative and critical appropriation with communities of faith, we can and should work together as all of us seek to interpret and also to shape our experience. In this collaborative enterprise, communities of faith and communities of learning inherit a shared sense of purpose from the past and have the prospect of a common agenda for the future.

———— 7

From Civil Religion to Public Faith

In this chapter I turn again to the questions of the role of religion in the broader society, this time with particular attention to issues involved in the relationship between religious and political life. First, I will offer my assessment of the general project that has come to be epitomized by the term "civil religion."[1] I use this term to refer to attempts to express a shared set of religious values in order to provide a common frame of reference for society as a whole. Because I find such attempts instructive even when the lessons are as much negative as positive, I will conduct an audit of what I take to be the assets and the liabilities of civil religion in this sense. Against the background of this balance sheet, I will, second, describe and evaluate the alternative to civil religion represented in appeals to the absolute authority of religious experience or revealed truth. Here, too, I will attempt to identify weaknesses as well as strengths. Third, I will sketch a chastened approach to civil religion that I term "public faith." In elaborating this approach I seek to appropriate the strengths of both civil religion and its critics while guarding against their weaknesses. Fourth and finally, I will offer an overview of the implications of this position for current debates about the relationship of religion to politics.

CIVIL RELIGION

The assets, strengths, or virtues of civil religion are very considerable. I note two: civil religion is intentionally public in character; and it represents an attempt to identify common ground among positions that may differ in significant particulars. Both of these virtues are impressive, and in American civil religion they mutually support and reinforce each other. But despite their close association in the United States, they are in principle separable and not infrequently separate in other contexts.

In the history of virtually all human societies, the public character of religion has been simply taken for granted. What has come to be called religion was the shared system of symbolic forms and acts, the myths and rituals, that interpreted and in turn shaped personal identity, social institutions, and cultural patterns. Such a system of symbols was pervasively present in public life even when it was not a focus of general awareness. In a culturally homogeneous traditional society, a common system of symbolic forms and acts provided the shared frame of reference for that society. But even when there was a recognized plurality of religious and cultural communities, by far the most common pattern in human history has been for a single tradition to occupy the position of the officially sanctioned religion. In short, religion has been publicly established—either as the taken-for-granted frame of reference of all members of the society or as the dominant religious position, in effect the religious counterpart of political authority, supported by the state and in turn providing legitimation for that state.

The institutionalization of religion in America stands in sharp contrast to this prevailing pattern in human history. The situation here is certainly not without significant antecedents and precedents. In particular, the American experiment is derived from two central developments of the European Reformation and Enlightenment: first, the splintering of Western Christendom into a plurality of distinct churches; and second, the growth of an intellectual tradition self-consciously critical of all the forms of ecclesiastical Christianity. But the American experiment does more than simply replicate or perpetuate this double inheritance. It expresses the implications of this pluralism and criticism in institutional terms. The result is the American rejection in principle of an established national church—in contrast to both homogeneous traditional cultures and societies that accord privileged or official status to only one or two religious communities.

This context of disestablishment of religion is what renders the intentionally public character of civil religion noteworthy. In societies in which religion is established, its public character may go without saying. But when religion is in principle not officially sanctioned and when multiple religious communities not only coexist but are defined as having equal societal status and when, finally, a tradition of criticism over against all religion is socially accepted, then the intentionally public character of religion is an attainment rather than a given.

This attainment must resist and overcome the temptations inherent in this context to construe religion in simply privatized terms. The forms of religion that succumb to this temptation are much in evidence: religion is only a matter of personal taste or preference; salvation has to do only with individual fulfillment either here and now or in the beyond hereafter; and so on. Over against such privatized interpretations of religious symbolism, civil religion insists on a role in shaping the values that undergird public life and in promoting a sense of social responsibility that transcends the interests of the individual. That, then, is a central strength of civil religion: its intentionally public character.

The second of the two virtues I note is the commitment of civil religion to identifying common ground among differing particular positions. The pluralism involved has certainly broadened and deepened over time. Among the founders of the country the range of positions taken into account was quite limited. Even radicals like Tom Paine were still strongly under Christian influence in arguing for a kind of unitarian deism. But the commitment in principle against every national establishment of religion not only protected other Christians against Anglicans or Calvinists but also set the precedent for a host of other communities, including in particular Jews (and now also Buddhists, Hindus, Muslims, and others), and also of course for so-called nonbelievers of all kinds.

In this context of increasingly radical pluralism, the attempt to discern common ground among quite different positions is enormously difficult but nonetheless unavoidable. To identify, express, and affirm shared values in and through quite different symbolic forms is a challenge that must be faced if a genuinely pluralistic society is to develop a workable polity. Accordingly, the commitment of civil religion to this task of fashioning and sustaining the fundamental values and institutional patterns common to the society as a whole is a significant strength.

As much as this discerning of common ground in and through

differences may be an asset, however, it also points to liabilities in civil religion. Two in particular are worth noting. The first is that in seeking common ground, civil religion too often reduces distinctive traditions to a least common denominator. The second is that in struggling to articulate fundamental values and institutional patterns for the society as a whole, civil religion may become an uncritical apologist for existing arrangements.

The first liability scarcely needs elaboration. Most of us are all too familiar with the pallid fare that results when religious commitments are reduced to a least common denominator. Think of the average council of churches or interfaith worship service. Such organizations and events no doubt serve definite purposes. But they are scarcely religiously vital or dynamic. Instead, they are frankly derivative and therefore unavoidably dependent on the particular communities being brought together. In attempting to encompass a wide range of ideas and attitudes, civil religion is always in danger of sacrificing the depth of particular commitment.

The second liability similarly follows from the attempt to be encompassing or inclusive. In seeking to express overall affirmations, civil religion may submerge minority positions or obscure underrepresented interests. In providing a sacred canopy for society as a whole, civil religion too often legitimates only established ideational traditions and social arrangements. Although underlying values and institutional commitments may have the potential for registering criticism and even resistance to prevailing patterns, this potential is not realized because of the actual power of established interests to shape the acceptable forms of civil religion. Indeed, because civil religion is not solidly grounded in particular religious communities, it may all too readily be appropriated and manipulated by political leaders seeking to provide legitimation for their own agenda.

To summarize, here is the balance sheet on civil religion as I have outlined it. On the positive side, there are two assets: first, civil religion is intentionally public in character; second, it seeks common ground among diverse positions. And on the negative side, there are two liabilities: first, civil religion may attain breadth at the expense of depth; second, it may lead to an erosion of the critical power of religious commitment over against the broader society. Against the background of this balance sheet, it is scarcely surprising that there is ambivalence about civil religion and that the quest for alternatives is both recurrent and persistent.

ABSOLUTE CLAIM

To counter the tendency of religion or theology to become subservient to the prevailing culture, religious individuals and communities characteristically appeal to the authority of religious insight or revelation. In its sharpest form, this appeal is to the unqualified or absolute authority of religious insight or revealed truth over against which all other standards are deemed decisively limited, inadequate, deficient, even perverse. Especially for those religious communities with a strong prophetic tradition, the attractions of standing staunchly over against established practice are quite strong. Those attractions are certainly resistible: even religious communities with strong prophetic traditions have all too frequently managed to ignore them in favor of accommodations with the prevailing culture. Still, appeal to an unassailable authority standing in judgment against the dominant tendencies of the broader society imbues religious commitment with a heady sense of purpose and an impressive social and cultural power. To thunder, "Thus saith the Lord," to assert, "The Bible says," or to pronounce a practice to be "a sin against the law of God" is to assume intrinsic religious authority. Not surprisingly, such authoritative appeals are very attractive in comparison to settling for the situation into which civil religion may degenerate—namely, the situation in which religious traditions provide only ornaments for a secular mass culture and consumer society. In contrast to this trap, religion based on appeal to unassailable authority has the double attraction of being both irreducibly particular and forcefully critical.

Probably the best-known twentieth-century instance of such criticism in Christian traditions is the 1934 Barmen Declaration, in which a federation of churches in Germany protested against the pretensions of Nazism. This eloquent confession is often cited as evidence of the prophetic power of appeals to divine revelation. It may accordingly be worth taking note of this instance in some detail.

The Barmen Declaration admirably exemplifies how religious authority that is sharply distinguished from secular culture may be invoked in opposition to the prevailing trends of that culture. In short, the Barmen Declaration expressed an eloquent and potent *No!* to its age. It articulated that rejection through appeal to sharply stated Christian confessions. The confessions were formulated as interpretations of specific verses from the Bible. Each verse is from the New Testament and was selected to authorize absolute and exclusive claims for Christ and the Christian church. The resultant affirmation in each case was in turn contrasted with what is rejected as false doctrine. Included in particular was the rejection of every claim that "events and powers, figures and truths" other than "the one Word of God" are "God's revelation." Also rejected was the attempt either to imbue the church with secular power or to arrogate to the state the role of "the single and total order of human life, thus fulfilling the church's vocation as well."[2]

As is evident from even this very cursory summary, the critical power of the Barmen Declaration was generated through appeals to the authority of the Word of God and the highly particular identity of the Christian church as differentiated from the broader culture. This critical power was enormously important. It represents the all-too-infrequent prophetic stance of religious truth over against the perversity of the secular or quasi-religious world. As such, it is an enduring testimony to the capacity of religious commitment to stand over against, to resist, the idolatry of every human authority that claims to be ultimate.

And yet even in and through the eloquence of testimony against the idolatry of human ideologies like Nazism, the limitations of this stance are also evident. Precisely because of the sharply focused particularity of its appeal, the Barmen Declaration was notably deficient in addressing issues beyond the assertion of the authority and the autonomy of the Christian church. The interests of the church were firmly registered. In allowing themselves to be co-opted by the Third Reich, the so-called German Christians were attacked for undermining the integrity of the Christian church. This hybrid of state and church was, therefore, to be resisted with the uncompromising fervor that grounding in the truth of revelation provided. The result was the assertion of the autonomous authority of the church of Christ—the federation of German Confessional Churches, Lutheran, Reformed, and United, bound together in this declaration of the German Evangelical Church. But beyond the assertion of the autonomy of this Evangelical Church, the Barmen Declaration was notably silent about other issues. Here the exclusive reliance on verses from the New Testament is indicative. Perhaps to avoid dissension within the various Protestant Christian communities, no appeal to the Hebrew Scriptures was included. Nor was there any condemnation of the increasingly blatant anti-Semitism of the Third Reich. Instead, the Barmen Declaration confined itself to appeals to the authorities of particular Christian communities and asserted the autonomy of the Christian church over against the so-called German Christian churches and their government-supported administrators.

Even in and through its eloquent testimony against the idolatrous glorification of secular or quasi-religious ideologies, the Barmen Declaration therefore illustrates inadequacies in reliance on appeals to particular authorities that are in principle alleged to be discontinuous with ordinary historical experience. Such appeals generate and conduct a sense of power for particular individuals and communities that are under assault. Because of the sharp disjunction between the transcendent authority invoked and the specific historical situation being threatened, such appeals too often do not, however, provide positive guidance for historical action outside the boundaries of the community whose interests and identity are being preserved.

Illustrations of this pattern are not, of course, confined to the Barmen Declaration and the theology associated with it. Instead, the pattern is a recurrent one across religious traditions. In stark form, it is illustrated in the discipline of ascetics, hermits, and monks who turn from entanglements in this world to focus on orientation to an ultimate reality at least distinguished from if not opposed to ordinary historical life. Think of Taoist recluses, Hindu ascetics, early Christian desert hermits, Theravada Buddhist or Catholic Christian solitary monks. There are of course also less austere examples of the pattern, as is evident in the myriad instances in the history of religions of widely held views that so concentrate on the goal of salvation in another realm that their dominant attitude toward secular life is one of rejection. All such positions share a critical stance over against historical attainments. But they also share a lack of interest in, inclination for, or capacity to shape historical life toward positive achievement or fulfillment.

To sum up, while appeals to the unqualified or absolute authority of religious insight or revelation are attractive in the critical power that they generate and conduct, such appeals are also deeply problematical on two grounds. First, there is the threat of a retreat to

private insight or exclusively particular awareness—a threat unavoidably entailed in the claim to have direct access to absolute truth,
access that is in principle different from all other human experience
and therefore discontinuous with such other experience and not
subject to generally accepted modes of understanding and evaluation. Second, there is the more pragmatic problem that the impulse
toward unqualified condemnation of society and certainly even
more the tendency toward undifferentiated rejection of the world
result in a lack of constructive guidance not substantially different
from the effects of secular relativism.

PUBLIC FAITH

In seeking to appropriate the strengths of both civil religion and
its critics while guarding against their weaknesses, it is initially
encouraging to note that each position in fact has substantial resources for countering the weaknesses of the other. The critical
power of appeals to the absolute authority of religious experience
or revealed truth offers a welcome contrast to the tendency in civil
religion to be shallow and uncritical. Conversely, the positive impulse of civil religion in seeking to be public in character and to
identify common ground among differing positions provides an
orientation that programmatically resists the tendency of authoritarian religion to retreat to private appeals that deliver too little
publicly accessible guidance for historical life, especially in pluralistic societies.

While the respective strengths of civil religion and its critics are
evident and also evidently in each case offer correctives to the
weaknesses of the other, the strengths themselves are not, however,
self-evidently compatible. The critical power of particular religious
conviction over against the broader society derives in significant
measure from its very particularity in insisting on the authority of
truth that is not accessible through the methods or in keeping with
the canons of ordinary knowing. Accordingly, this strength of the
critical power of particular religion is not incidentally but rather
systematically opposed to the positive impulses of civil religion in
seeking to be public and to affirm common ground among different
positions.

The central question to be addressed in attempting to sketch a chastened approach to civil religion is, therefore, how commitment may be both particular and public—how it may seek common ground in the public arena while at the same time generating and conducting the critical power of particular religion. This question is of more than only theoretical interest. In an era that is witnessing serious erosion of consensus about common or shared values, it also assumes great practical import, as is evident in debates concerning the role of religion in political life.

Commitment that is both particular and public in principle rejects the two easiest and probably most frequent resolutions of the tensions entailed in this set of issues. It rejects the reduction of religion to a least common denominator allegedly shared by all. At the same time, it refuses to confine religion to the private sphere. In this double rejection, public faith parts company with religious liberals who advocate toleration as a sufficient response to pluralism and with secular humanists who prefer to keep religion altogether out of such domains as economics and politics.

The distinctiveness of public faith so construed is perhaps most evident in the ways it exercises critical power over against the broader society. It may appeal to the particular traditions of its own community—its stories or teachings or injunctions. But it recognizes that those traditions are not authoritative apart from their capacity to illuminate and their power to shape public issues that confront adherents and nonadherents alike. This requirement of accessibility to others does not mean that only common or shared traditions may be appropriately invoked. It does, however, preclude the imposition of standards or obligations that are advocated exclusively on the basis of appeals to allegedly absolute authorities.

The critical power of appeals to religious authority derives from their claim to represent transcendent truth over against the ways of the world. Hence even when those appeals are expressed in highly particular forms, they invoke the authority of universal truth. Analogously, insofar as civil religion is critical, it appeals to norms, principles, or ideals that inform but also transcend the best practice of a particular society. In this case as well, there is reference to transcending value or universal truth. Public faith also enlists this power of appeal to the transcendent and the universal. But it does so with greater awareness of the need for leverage against the characteristic provincialisms to which civil religion and religious authoritarianism are prone.

The provincialism to which civil religion is prone results from its tendency to reflect and in turn to legitimate the values of the society for which it provides a general frame of reference. Because civil religion attempts to identify common ground among positions that may differ in significant particulars, it is in intention less provincial than the traditions among which it mediates. For example, insofar as American civil religion succeeds in articulating values shared by Protestants of many denominations and perhaps also by Catholics and Jews, it at least initially seems less provincial than, say, humanist (as distinguished from theist and Christian) Unitarian-Universalism, Trappist monasticism, or Hassidic Judaism. But this intention to be inclusive in one or more respects may too easily obscure the provincialism inherent in the very attempt to provide a frame of reference for one specific society, in this case the United States of America. In sum, the aim of encompassing several religious traditions within a single nation in effect accentuates the features of the national identity that those religious traditions have in common.

Unlike civil religion, appeals to the absolute authority of religious experience or revealed truth have no intrinsic or necessary relationship to a single society or nation. Such appeals are not intrinsically provincial in a geographical sense. Indeed, great missionary religions—Buddhism, Christianity, and Islam, to take the three most powerful instances in human history—have a universalistic thrust that is a substantial resource for countering every such geographical provincialism. But precisely this universalizing missionary thrust in turn entails the threat of its own provincialism: a cultural or symbolic provincialism rather than a natural or geographical one. This provincialism results from the presumption of direct access to absolute truth, access typically (though not invariably) restricted to those who attain the same standpoint or follow the same approach and interpret that standpoint or approach with reference to the same set of symbols.

Public faith must resist both the national provincialism of civil religion and the cultural provincialism of religious authoritarianism. It can do so by building on the sound instincts that civil religion and appeals to the absolute authority of particular religions have in countering their own characteristic provincialisms. But it can then also reinforce those positive tendencies by affirming the criticism that each has of the other.

Civil religion at its best guards against the threat of national idolatry through appeals to transcending value or universal truth that stands in judgment over the pretensions and the collective self-interest of the nation. In short, even civil religion is not without its prophets. The figure of Abraham Lincoln—perhaps the foremost exemplar of American civil religion—is eloquent testimony to this capacity for national self-criticism in civil religion. So there are resources within the traditions of civil religion for countering the tendency toward uncritical glorification of the nation. Because public faith is not committed to seeking a least common denominator, it may, however, also invoke the particular traditions of its own community, including specifically commitments to a universalism that transcends every provincial society, as a further reinforcement of resistance to national idolatries of every sort. Thus, despite disagreements on other grounds, public faith shares with authoritarian religion the capacity to appeal to highly particular traditions that are universal in scope and therefore relativize the absolutist pretensions of any single nation.

This capacity to resist the human temptation to self-glorification is a great strength of particular religion. Too often this critical capacity is not, however, extended to rigorous self-criticism. The result is an absolutizing of one historically relative tradition of interpretation in one religious community and an insistence that this authoritative position may not appropriately be subjected to critical and comparative scrutiny. At this point public faith parts company with authoritarian religion. It maintains that every position including its own must in principle allow for the most uncompromising criticism (including especially self-criticism) and comparative assessment. Through such public interchange with other communities the characteristic provincialism of authoritarian religion—namely, its tendency toward absolutizing its own perspective—may be countered. And only on the basis of such public interaction among multiple religious as well as secular communities may increasingly adequate expressions of public faith be developed in a pluralistic world.

Public faith may, then, be both particular and public only because it is also committed to critical and comparative inquiry. Through critical and comparative interaction with its counterparts in both religious and secular traditions, public faith seeks more adequate expressions of its own commitments. At the same time, the relative adequacy of its diagnoses and prescriptions is the basis on which it commends its positions. This relative adequacy in interpreting and shaping an increasingly shared global experience is the authority to which particular commitment appeals in the public arena—an authority that provides a common court of appeal for all such particular claims.

RELIGION AND POLITICS

I am aware that this sketch of public faith is at a sufficiently high level of abstraction that it may seem quite removed from actual debates as to the appropriate role of religion in civic affairs. I will, therefore, conclude this chapter with a brief overview of how I see the implications of this conception of public faith for the relationship of religion to politics. This overview will at the same time provide a final set of contrasts to both civil religion and religious authoritarianism.

The conception of public faith as I have sketched it implies a twofold principle to guide reflection on the relationship of religion and politics. First, government should in no way whatsoever either support or suppress particular religious positions as such. Second, religiously committed individuals and institutions should be entirely free to participate in whatever ways they choose in the full range of political expression and organization. This formulation is deliberately asymmetrical: there should be a wall of separatism between church and state; but it should block traffic in only one direction. Put less metaphorically, while government should not interfere with religious life, religion can and should shape political deliberations.

Pressure to transgress the first tenet of this twofold principle is exerted from various quarters. Civil religion violates it insofar as it tends not only to align a common religious orientation with the political order but also to enlist government in support of specific religious positions. But so, too, do religious communities that seek government sanction for their particular views. The issue of prayer in the public schools of the United States illustrates this tendency— whether it is a quite particular prayer like the Lord's Prayer or a very general prayer that might include at least some Hindus, Muslims, and Jews, as well as Christians. In either case, enlisting state support for religious observance transgresses the first tenet of this twofold principle, to the disservice of religion as well as politics.

The second tenet of this twofold principle simply recognizes how unacceptable it is to religiously committed people to expect that their deepest convictions will not influence their political behavior. To insist that religiously committed individuals and institutions be free to participate in political life in whatever ways they choose does not entail approbation for any and every form of such participation. It does, however, recognize that religious individuals and institutions must themselves be allowed to determine the modes of participation they deem appropriate. So, for example, black churches may well continue their long-established practice of endorsing specific candidates for office and even of serving as a base for political organizing. To take other instances, religious leaders are entirely free to express their views on the implications of their various traditions on such public issues as racial justice, appropriate health care, welfare funding, foreign aid, nuclear arms, and abortion.

This general formulation of the twofold principle that guides public faith in reflecting on the relationship of religion to politics still leaves a host of decisions unresolved as religious individuals and communities confront specific issues. But those unresolved decisions are properly located in the deliberations of religious communities rather than in the political process. It may be that most religious leaders and institutions are well-advised to resist endorsements of individual candidates. But that is a decision for them to make, not one to be forced on them through political disenfranchisement. Similarly, religious communities may decide against taking firm positions on public issues that are hotly contested and on which their own members are sharply divided. But this question also is one for religious communities themselves to decide.

There is no doubt that the presence of religion in public life can and usually does heighten the intensity of debate in ways that too often block resolution of pressing issues. That fact enhances the attractiveness of banning religion from the public arena. But the cost of completely privatizing religion is too high a price to pay for the benefit of greater tranquility in public affairs.

We are becoming more and more acutely aware of how costly it is to settle for public life divorced from the questions of meaning and value central to religious commitment. Influential religious and political leaders are prepared to trade in the currency that perhaps a majority of our fellow citizens accept as their own. The dangers of inadequate civil religion are, however, evident in such commerce: an uncritical celebration of the dominant traditions of the nation to the exclusion of critical or subordinated voices.

Over against this homogenizing and triumphalist tendency, what we need is public faith: commitment, whether religious or secular, that is unapologetically particular because it recognizes its roots in definite communities, traditions, and values but that is also entirely public because it is committed to comparative and critical inquiry. That is a tall order. It certainly would be easier if we had a single set of symbols that all of us agreed in finding both rich and compelling. But that is not the case. Accordingly, nothing less than something like the tougher stance of public faith will do if we are to continue to have—or perhaps better: to reestablish—a society with public purposes beyond individual gratification.

8

Communities of Commitment

In this concluding chapter, I will attempt a final drawing together of the themes of commitment and community in the context of societies that, like ours, combine powerful strains of individualism and pluralism with increasingly complex and impersonal market forces and bureaucratic processes. To that end, I will develop a single line of argument in four stages. First, I will sketch the modern Western impulse toward emancipation from captivity to tradition and indicate how this freedom has become as much a negative as a positive tendency in our society because impersonal market forces and bureaucratic processes have displaced more traditional patterns of relationship. Second, I will note that the prevalence of such impersonal market forces and bureaucratic processes in our society engenders a nostalgic yearning for what is idealized as the direct and personal experience of intimate and stable communities. Third, in an attempt to specify further what is at stake in this idealization of traditional communities in contrast to modern pluralistic societies, I will examine the conception of social practice as it is illustrated in several domains of contemporary experience. Finally, I will seek to show how such social practices and the communities that express and sustain them may provide critical leverage over against complacency about contemporary society without indulging in nostalgic idealization of tradition.

FREEDOM FROM TRADITION

In the modern West, we are the heirs of a several-hundred-year-old tradition that, paradoxically, has aimed to deliver us from captivity to traditions. This emancipation from the hold of traditions was and is central to the self-understanding of the generations that termed their century the Enlightenment. Writing toward the end of that century, in 1784, the philosopher Immanuel Kant expressed eloquently and succinctly what he and his generation intended with the designation they claimed as their own: "Enlightenment is humanity's release from its self-incurred tutelage."[1] Kant articulated in words what he became convinced the French Revolution a few years later embodied in deeds: liberation from both ideas and institutionalized practices that had outlived their usefulness.

The impulse to liberate us from the captivity of traditions is paradoxical because this impulse has itself become a very potent tradition. This tradition certainly did not begin from scratch with the Enlightenment. It has important antecedents in the economic, political, and especially religious patterns of previous centuries in the West—and also intriguing analogues in other cultures. But this tradition of freedom from tradition is a pervasive influence embodied in our social institutions and personal behavior to an unprecedented degree.

We can understand the development of this tradition over the past several hundred years only if we see its interconnections within the central institutional patterns of the modern West: market capitalism; democratic political processes; contractual relations as the basis for the legal system; voluntary associations as a characteristic form of social organization. One effect of this interconnected set of developments has indeed been to allow an unprecedented degree of latitude for individual initiative and choice. Over time, increasing numbers of people have had larger measures of freedom to choose among personal relationships, lines of work, places to live, associations to join, and leisure activities.

This increasing freedom from traditionally ascribed identities, associations, and activities is correlative with the development of the other institutional patterns of the modern West because those other patterns in effect provide new modes of relating individuals to each other to replace the previously taken-for-granted relationships of premodern traditions. Foremost among those new modes is an increasing reliance on patterns that in principle treat all individuals equally. All people are in principle equal before the law. Every individual who counts as a political person in principle has one vote. People in principle may join associations to which they choose to belong. Market mechanisms in principle respond to whatever is their medium of exchange, regardless of the individuals involved. To be sure, equal treatment was not always realized in practice, a very significant failure socially and morally. But that failure notwithstanding, modern Western societies have developed procedures and institutional forms that are impersonal in the sense that they relate people to each other in ways that are in principle independent of individual differences.

This development of institutional patterns that in principle treat all individuals equally is a glorious achievement and is appropriately celebrated as liberating, as an emancipation, as allowing unprecedented freedom. At the same time, however, such patterns unavoidably tend to standardize individuals insofar as they relate people to each other through impersonal mechanisms. Markets are no doubt the most efficient instances of such mechanisms. But bureaucracies that are required to follow impersonal rules of procedure also illustrate the tendency to develop modes of relationship that treat individuals equally. In sum, with increasing freedom from traditionally defined roles, individuals become more or less interchangeable and therefore are related to each other through market mechanisms or other institutional patterns for which individual characteristics are irrelevant.

I doubt that I have to belabor the extent to which our society represents an advanced stage of this line of development. We are confronted with an enormous range of choices in geographical location, career, personal associations, life-style. Yet we all too often are related to each other as more or less interchangeable parts. Granted, opinion polls cannot interview a single person and generalize from there. But a strikingly small sample will do. Granted, advertising takes account of market segments. But within specifiable boundary conditions, behavior is remarkably predictable. Granted, political candidates do not treat the entire electorate as an undifferentiated group. But a limited number of quite definite voting blocks can be specified.

In response to this domination of our public life by more or less impersonal patterns of relationship, many of us retreat to the personal satisfactions of our private lives. If we find intimate communities increasingly displaced by impersonal bureaucracies and market mechanisms, then we turn the more resolutely to families.

If our work is more and more routinized and subjected to regulation, we invest more of our time and energy and other resources in our leisure activities. Yet even here, the paradoxical union of free choice and interchangeability confronts us. Family members also are liberated from traditional roles and therefore insist—rightly—that they all be treated equally. Similarly, leisure activities are no less subject to marketing than are other commodities. In short, our consumerism standardizes us even in and through the range of options proffered to us.

YEARNING FOR COMMUNITY

Faced with the tendency toward a society of separate individuals related to each other through impersonal market forces and bureaucratic processes, the temptation is to succumb to powerful bouts of nostalgia. We idealize that wonderful bygone age in which members of intimate and stable communities related to each other directly and personally. People knew each other. They had shared values. They trusted each other. They treated each other with respect. They rejoiced in each other's achievements and comforted each other in times of trial and sorrow. When someone was in need, neighbors pitched in and helped out. Perhaps most important, people were not viewed as bits of data supporting generalizations, interchangeable parts, or impersonal atoms. Instead, they were in direct and personal contact as individuals with all their particularities, not to say peculiarities or idiosyncrasies.

Even so brief an evocation of this bygone age suggests that much has been lost in the transition to our market-oriented and bureaucratic society. Of course, those small communities were often provincial and narrow. Of course, they were quite homogeneous and insisted on conformity whenever even small deviations from established mores developed. Of course, those communities also exemplify conflict, struggle for personal advantage, violence. Of course, statistical generalizations across subsets of the population by status, gender, occupation, and income would also in principle be possible for those communities. To be blunt, no such idealized past age of intimate community ever existed. Yet even with all of those entirely accurate and appropriate qualifications, much has been lost in the transition from communities that allowed and even required a degree of direct personal contact only rarely achieved in advanced industrial societies.

More traditional communities had a sense of time and space different from ours. This sense of time and space need not be explicitly stated or even conscious. Indeed, it is all the more powerful when it is simply taken for granted. Members of traditional communities share a continuity over time together with the sharply focused location in space that their small scale allows. As a result, neighbors know each other closely and for long periods—entire lifetimes or even multiple generations. In contrast, most of us shift locations frequently and have quite wide-ranging networks of acquaintances. In comparison to our more traditional forebears, we therefore have a much larger-scale spatial or geographical orientation and a much shorter time horizon for any specific place.

In the modern West—and especially in America—there are, then, many more people than ever before in human history who have moved often and have far more acquaintances than close friends. (Note that this very phrase—close friend—works metaphorically only if proximity implies intimacy.) Precisely those of us in this situation, no matter how much we value mobility and personal freedom, also feel the pull, the attraction, of membership in an intimate and caring community that allows direct personal contact and embodies a sense of continuity, a reliable identity, over time. Think of the impulse to seek out roots—an impulse that our culture in turn appropriates and packages as one more artifact in our global shopping center. Or more personally, for those of us who have moved often, think of our own (admittedly also ambivalent) response to returning to our home towns.

This nostalgia is not merely a personal and private reaction. It also exerts a pervasive influence on our public life. Appeals to it are especially common in politics and religion. The ethical standards of the rural community or the small town are evoked to counter the corrosive effect of the big city and its large-scale institutions, including especially big government and the omnipresent media. In recent years, we have witnessed a similar development in discussions of education. There is of course the perennial analogue of idealizations of the small and intimate undergraduate college over against the bureaucratic and impersonal large university. Less frequent is the appeal to a core of common learning over against

the incoherent assortment of offerings in the cafeteria of the mul-
tiversity. But we have recently been treated to the spectacle of best-
sellerdom for Allan Bloom's *The Closing of the American Mind*, a book
far more frequently bought than read but still an intriguing con-
firmation of the attraction of appeals to a common set of traditions
that provide a collective sense of identity and continuity over time.[2]

I have elaborated our nostalgia for the past because I think it
important that we acknowledge the truth of its appeal and also its
limitations. We need to be aware of our own attraction to the
idealization of intimate community and continuity of identity over
time. At the same time, we must recognize that even if approxi-
mations of such communities existed in the past, they are inadequate as models for our corporate life today not only because they
are irretrievable but also because their insistence on conformity is
morally ambiguous in the context of pluralism like that of modern
Western societies. To sum up: we are aware of the deficiencies of
our consumer society and mass culture, with its all-but-exclusive
reliance on impersonal market forces and bureaucratic processes;
this sense of the inadequacy of our world renders us susceptible
to nostalgia for what we at least imagine to be the direct and
personal experience of intimate and stable communities in the past;
yet at the same time we also must acknowledge that the attempt
to live in that past is an exercise in self-delusion.

SOCIAL PRACTICE

What then are our choices? Either complacency in assaying contemporary life or nostalgia for an irretrievable past? Put still more
sharply, either self-indulgence in our consumer society and mass
culture or self-delusion in a false idealization of communal life?

The inadequacies of the alternatives mandate a more differentiated approach, an approach that allows distinctions within the
overall contrast between modern pluralistic societies and more traditional communities. A set of distinctions that I find helpful in
sorting out variables is one that has developed largely out of con-
versations around a book published in 1981, Alasdair MacIntyre's
After Virtue.[3] The conception that I find illuminating is that of a
social practice. A social practice is an activity that aims at and
realizes goods, values, or benefits internal to the activity itself. The

intended contrast is to the achievement of external goods, values, or benefits—prestige or money, for example—that have no necessary relationship to the standards of excellence intrinsic to the activity itself. The settings that allocate such external goods are institutions, which in turn are necessary to support social practices but in principle are distinguishable from them.

Some examples will, I hope, serve to clarify this set of distinctions. What may seem a trivial illustration is probably nonetheless the clearest: athletics. A sport like football is a social practice insofar as it realizes goods, values, or benefits internal to its own activity. Such internal goods include disciplined training, rigorously developed teamwork, sustained concentration, exemplary physical capacities, and so on. This social practice is more than simply a collection of skills, though in its highest exemplifications it certainly presupposes very impressive abilities. It is also distinguished from an institution, even if highly complex institutional arrangements accompany and support it.

I certainly do not have to belabor the fact that the social practice of athletics not only has the potential to contribute benefits but also may all too readily be corrupted. This corruption of a sport like football or any other social practice occurs when external goods—money, status, power—displace internal goods as the motives and goals of the activity. The corrosive effects of such displacement of internal by external goods has become all too evident in recent years in both professional and collegiate athletics. Accordingly, the conception of athletics as a social practice intentionally counters the domination of sports by commercial interests and instead focuses on its intrinsic value as disciplined activity aimed at achieving excellence in terms of its own rules and standards.

Another illustration of a social practice—one that is not susceptible of trivialization in the ways that athletics may be—is medical care. Like athletics, medicine requires the development of highly refined skills that are indispensable to its practice. Through such skills as empathetic caring and astute diagnosis, doctors and nurses pursue goods, values, or benefits internal to the practice of medicine. Healing and health or well-being, to describe those goods in the most general terms, are pursued as intrinsic to the practice of medical care, as definitive of the identity of medical professionals, as in turn evoking the virtues or forms of excellence required for those roles.

In our society, this practice of medical care is deeply embedded in such institutions as hospitals, governmental and private insurance and reimbursement systems, universities, medical proprietary groups, health maintenance organizations, various professional associations, and so on. Such institutions are in effect the bearers of medical care as a social practice. The institutional bearers of medical care are unavoidably involved in acquiring resources and distributing money, power, and status. They cannot do otherwise if they are to sustain not only themselves as institutions but also the medical care of which they are the bearers. But while such institutions play an indispensable role, they also pose a direct threat to the social practice that they support because they may come to be dominated by their necessary involvement with attracting and allocating resources. Thus such external goods as money, power, and status, goods that have no intrinsic relation to medical care as a social practice, may compete with and in extreme instances undermine or corrupt goods internal to medicine itself—as, for example, when patients urgently in need of attention are turned away from hospital emergency rooms because they do not have adequate verification of medical insurance.

A third instance of social practice illustrates the same crosscurrents. Education, like athletics and medicine, is a social practice in that it pursues goods, values, or benefits internal to its own activity. In this case as well, institutional settings are crucial for the support of a social practice—and those settings, in their attraction and allocation of external goods, may in effect serve to undermine the practice of education that they intend to support. But education as a social practice is distinguishable from those institutional arrangements and is pursued only insofar as its aim is to realize the internal goods of disciplined teaching and learning in principle apart from their relation to such external goods as compensation for faculty and job training or career prospects for students.

BEYOND COMPLACENCY AND NOSTALGIA

Social practices like athletics, medical care, and education are, to repeat, deeply embedded in their respective institutional settings. Beyond those particular institutions, they are also located within the array of market forces and bureaucratic processes that structures our society as a whole. But within that set of relationships, social practices provide crucial leverage against allowing every transaction to be determined by market or bureaucratic allocation of such external goods as money, power, and status.

That social practices define their own internal goods, values, or benefits provides this leverage. Only insofar as athletics has its own internal standards of excellence can it resist being completely engulfed by market forces that allocate rewards to individuals in competition with each other in terms of considerations that may have more to do with entertainment or marketing than with athletics as a social practice. Similarly, doctors and nurses must concentrate on the pursuit of medical care in order to resist the pressures to subordinate the internal goods of their practice entirely to the market forces and bureaucratic processes that increasingly dominate our health care system.

So, too, teachers must counter the push so to accommodate education to market demand or bureaucratic requirements that the internal goods, values, or benefits of teaching and learning are undermined. Certainly teachers are not indifferent about, and in any case cannot ignore, the employment prospects of their students. Indeed, they may well argue that the most effective preparation for the most interesting careers is the broadest and most fundamental education because for such positions technical competence alone is not enough. But attractive and important as such arguments may be, they are inadequate to the challenge of preserving education as a social practice because they refer primarily to external goods rather than to the very actions of teaching and learning themselves. Instead of relying on arguments that tacitly accept the primacy of external goods, defenses of the practice of education must be grounded on the indispensability of its internal goods: disciplined mastery of method and subject so as to allow continuing excitement in discovery and creation.

Athletics, medicine, and education are of course not the only domains of our common life in which social practices provide leverage over against the market forces and bureaucratic processes that dominate our society. Perhaps the most visible and crucial other domain that cries out for the integrity of social practice as a counter to pervasive corruption is our political life. Here we all have a pressing shared interest in nurturing the values that social practices represent. Governance is a social practice insofar as it pursues the common good rather than personal gain as an end in itself. Like athletics, medicine, and education, politics is unavoidably embedded in institutions that collect and distribute resources on a massive scale. Precisely for that reason we must cultivate the social practice of governance aimed at the common good and work with and in communities devoted to embodying that practice. Without this ideal of governance and action to realize it, we will have only a further development of political patterns in which the exclusive motives and goals are accumulating money, power, and status.

A final example of social practice is in the domain at the heart of this study as a whole, namely, religion. Indeed, religious life and thought provide strikingly vivid illustrations of both social practices and their corruption. Throughout the religious literature of the world there are denunciations of false piety—of piety paraded in public to gain recognition and approbation. This corruption of religion is contrasted to worship or discipline directed to the divine or the ultimate and service intended to meet the needs of others. Such worship, discipline, and service are social practices: they realize goods, values, or benefits internal to their own activity in that they have the effect of extending the relationships and deepening the sensibilities of participants.

Like other social practices, worship, discipline, and service are embedded in institutions that collect and distribute resources. Like their secular counterparts, religious institutions may undermine the social practices of which they are bearers. They may, for example, allow considerations of financial gain, influence, or visibility to determine behavior irrespective of their impact on worship, dicipline, and service. But religious institutions, again like their secular counterparts, also play an indispensable role in supporting social practices. Indeed, the examples of worship, discipline, and service provide an especially compelling illustration of how crucial a community of shared commitment is to expressing and sustaining social practices.

Those of us who are members of religious communities certainly are or at least should be aware of the ever-present threat of false piety, of the corruption of religious practices. Yet we also affirm worship, discipline, and service as intrinsically worthwhile, as ends in themselves, as activities that entail internal goods, values, or benefits. In those practices, we catch a glimpse of our being delivered from our endless self-preoccupation and embraced in a new community. To use Christian imagery, it is membership in a new reality: baptism into the dying and rising Christ and eucharistic incorporation into the brokenness and wholeness of the divine-human body.

When it is vivid and vital, this sense of membership in a particular community imbues a sense of personal identity that is a crucial resource in confronting the depersonalizing pressures of modern societies. In this respect religious communities illustrate a pattern that is also exemplified in other domains. Precisely insofar as they provide leverage over against the more or less impersonal market forces and bureaucratic processes that increasingly dominate our society, all social practices presuppose and in turn foster communities that resist those dominant social tendencies. Those communities may be elusive and inchoate. For example, teams of relief workers struggling to deliver emergency assistance during a natural disaster may form such a community, the more so if they find themselves bound together in battling bureaucratic red tape and market-driven economic constraints. Communities that support social practices may, of course, also be more structured, as in professional organizations dedicated to protecting the quality of a service or voluntary associations devoted to preserving human rights. But in each case, to be viable, a social practice requires a community that nurtures it within the various institutional settings in which it is conducted.

The communities that are the correlates of contemporary social practices are certainly not the intimate and stable settings that our nostalgia conjures up from the past. Instead, even though they typically are grounded in deeply rooted traditions, the communities that nurture social practices may be mobile and open. They are, therefore, far more viable in a society that in principle rejects determinations of membership based exclusively on accidents of history and geography. At the same time, in social practices themselves there is the kind of direct and personal experience so often missing in societies dominated by markets and bureaucracies. Communities of social practice pursue activities aimed at realizing or achieving goods, values, or benefits that all participants affirm. Such cooperative activity in pursuit of shared values is all too rare in our society. That fact alone is a powerful reason to seek to enhance and extend the contexts in which social practices are pursued as we seek alternatives beyond complacency and nostalgia.

Specifically in the case of religious communities, the dangers of complacency and nostalgia are amply represented. Insofar as the sense of membership in a particular community is vivid and vital, it may nurture the capacity to stand over against the prevailing tendencies of the broader society and thereby provide a measure of resistance to complacency. But this particular identity may in turn all the more readily succumb to bouts of nostalgia. It is therefore also crucial that religious communities resist the temptation simply to turn in on themselves. Here, too, religious communities command substantial resources. To focus again on Christian imagery, the particular identity of membership in the body of Christ at the same time entails citizenship in a community that is universal in a double sense: it is in principle open to the participation of all, Jew or Greek, slave or free, male or female; and it is ultimately focused on that finally all-inclusive community to which Jesus pointed with his parables about the kingdom or commonwealth of God.

This universal thrust of religious imagery authorizes engagement in the broader society. In the language of the Protestant Reformation, it testifies to the priesthood of all believers as they pursue their secular as well as religious vocations. Consequently, religious communities can and should contribute to the broader society not only in nurturing their own worship, discipline, and service but also in seeking ways to foster social practices in other institutional settings. This contribution requires collaboration with other communities—informal as well as official, secular as well as religious—that support social practices. In a pluralistic society, this collaboration is entirely appropriate and also indispensable as diverse communities resist complete domination by market forces and bureaucratic processes. To close with a final testimony from Christian commitment, this collaboration may also hope to participate in the movement toward inclusive and transforming community that incorporates but also transcends every particular community, certainly not excepting the churches: the reality of God.

Notes

1. COMMITMENT AS APPROPRIATION OF TRADITIONS

1. As quoted in Robert N. Bellah, *Beyond Belief: Essays on Religion in a Post-Traditional World* (New York: Harper & Row, 1970), 43. Bellah's line of argument in the essay entitled "Religious Evolution" and in particular his discussion of "Modern Religion" (39–43) delineate this development of individualism in the post–Enlightenment West.

2. This dependence is strikingly evident in Mary Daly, *Beyond God the Father* (Boston: Beacon Press, 1973).

2. COMMUNITY AND DIVINITY

1. G. W. F. Hegel, *The Phenomenology of Mind*, trans. J. B. Baillie (New York: Harper & Row, 1967), 781–82; *Glauben und Wissen* in *Erste Druckschriften*, ed. Georg Lasson (Leipzig: Verlag von Felix Meiner, 1928), 345–46. Hegel in turn was of course quite consciously echoing both Luther and Christian liturgical traditions.

2. Friedrich Nietzsche, *Thus Spake Zarathustra*, trans. Thomas Common, in *The Philosophy of Nietzsche*, ed. Willard Huntington Wright (New York: Random House, Modern Library, 1954), 6.

3. Alfred North Whitehead, *Religion in the Making* (Cleveland: World Publishing, Meridian Books, 1965), 16.

4. Anselm of Canterbury, *Proslogium*, II–III, in *St. Anselm: Basic Writings*, trans. S. N. Deane (La Salle: Open Court, 1962), 7–9.

5. Althanasius, *On the Incarnation of the Word*, 54, in *Christology of the Later Fathers*, ed. Edward R. Hardy (Philadelphia: Westminster Press, 1954), 107.

3. CHRISTOLOGY IN THE CONTEXT OF PLURALISM

1. John Calvin, *Institutes of the Christian Religion*, I.i.1, ed. John T. McNeill (Philadelphia: Westminster Press, 1960), 35.

2. For an extended development of this argument that christological variables may be correlated with analogous distinctions in other traditions, see my *Christologies and Cultures: Toward a Typology of Religious Worldviews* (The Hague: Mouton Press, 1974).

3. J. N. D. Kelley, *Early Christian Creeds* (New York: Longmans, Green & Co., 1950), 297.

4. For a survey of the historical data and an argument for their relevance to contemporary spiritual discipline, see Margaret R. Miles, *Fullness of Life: Historical Foundations for a New Asceticism* (Philadelphia: Westminster Press, 1981).

4. THEOLOGY AND THE COMPARATIVE HISTORY OF RELIGIONS

1. The convergence is a renewed one in a double sense. First, as I note in the course of this chapter, what have become the two disciplines of theology and the history of religions have for most of human history in most cultural contexts not been sharply distinguished. Second, by the end of the nineteenth century, the two disciplines were increasingly related to each other and more recently display a renewed convergence only because of the forceful separation imposed on them by the influence of Neo-orthodoxy in Protestantism. On this latter point, see my *"Culture-Protestantism": German Liberal Theology at the Turn of the Twentieth Century* (Atlanta: Scholars Press for the American Academy of Religion, 1977).

2. Wilfred Cantwell Smith, in whose honor I wrote the essay from which this chapter has been adapted, has devoted a lifetime of thought and experience to understanding and interpreting this development. For an overview of his position, which over the years has influenced my own thinking very considerably, see *Towards a World Theology: Faith and the Comparative History of Religion* (Philadelphia: Westminster Press, 1981).

3. For a more extended consideration of this complex set of issues, see my *Beyond Existentialism and Zen: Religion in a Pluralistic World* (New York: Oxford University Press, 1979), esp. 9–26.

5. THE CHANGING ROLE OF RELIGION IN SOCIETY

1. For a fascinating delineation of the tensions intrinsic to this orientation, see G. W. F. Hegel's description of the "unhappy consciousness" in *The Phenomenology of Mind*, trans. J. B. Baillie (New York: Harper & Row, 1967), 251–67. The classic sociological formulations of this stance of world rejection are in the writings of Max Weber; see, e.g., *The Sociology of Religion*, trans. Ephraim Fischoff (Boston: Beacon Press, 1964), 166–245; "Religious Rejections of the World and Their Directions," in *From Max Weber: Essays in Sociology*, trans. H. H. Gerth and C. Wright Mills (New York: Oxford University Press, 1958), 323–59. (The last word in the title might better be translated as "ramifications," inasmuch as Weber examines the different areas in which world rejection has a bearing or implications.)

2. The classic description of this orientation of so-called primitive religion is Emile Durkheim, *The Elementary Forms of Religious Life*, trans. Joseph Ward Swain (New York: Collier Books, 1961). For references to more recent

studies and also for a schematic delineation of the similarities to and differences from both post-Enlightenment tendencies and the pattern of world rejection, see Robert N. Bellah, "Religious Evolution," in *Beyond Belief: Essays on Religion in a Post-Traditional World* (New York: Harper & Row, 1970), 20–50.

6. COMMUNITIES OF FAITH/
COMMUNITIES OF LEARNING

1. Immanuel Kant, *Critique of Pure Reason*, trans. Norman Kemp Smith (New York: Macmillan Co., 1963), 29.

2. Karl Barth, *The Epistle to the Romans*, trans. Edwyn C. Hoskyns (New York: Oxford University Press, 1972), esp. 240–317.

3. For what is probably the most concise statement of this line of criticism, see G. W. F. Hegel, *The Phenomenology of Mind*, trans. J. B. Baillie (New York: Harper & Row, 1967), 131–45.

7. FROM CIVIL RELIGION TO PUBLIC FAITH

1. For the last twenty years in this country, Robert N. Bellah's 1966 paper "Civil Religion in America" has figured prominently in this discussion. See *Beyond Belief: Essays on Religion in a Post-Traditional World* (New York: Harper & Row, 1970), 168–89. For more recent formulations, see Robert N. Bellah and Phillip E. Hammond, *Varieties of Civil Religion* (San Francisco: Harper & Row, 1980).

2. "Barmen Theological Declaration," in Rolf Ahlers, *The Barmen Theological Declaration of 1934: The Archeology of a Confessional Text* (Lewiston: Edwin Mellon Press, 1986), 39–42; the specific phrases quoted are on pp. 40, 42.

8. COMMUNITIES OF COMMITMENT

1. "What Is Enlightenment?" in *Kant on History*, ed. Lewis White Beck (Indianapolis: Bobbs-Merrill, 1963), 3.

2. Allan Bloom, *The Closing of the American Mind* (New York: Simon & Schuster, 1987).

3. Alasdair MacIntyre, *After Virtue* (Notre Dame, Ind.: University of Notre Dame Press, 1981). My discussion of social practices is indebted to Jeffrey Stout's article, "Liberal Society and the Language of Morals," *Soundings: An Interdisciplinary Journal* 69 (Spring/Summer 1986): esp. 51–56.

Index